BATTLE IN THE
ARCTIC SEAS

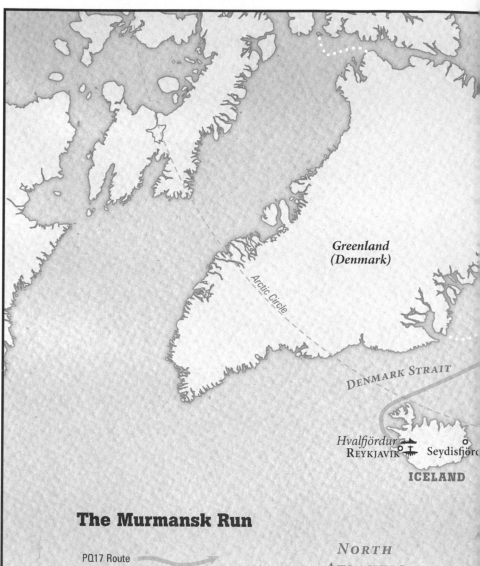

Greenland
(Denmark)

Arctic Circle

DENMARK STRAIT

Hvalfjördur
REYKJAVIK Seydisfjörd

ICELAND

The Murmansk Run

PQ17 Route

Allied Air Base

Allied Naval Base

Axis Air Base

Axis Naval Base

NORTH
ATLANTIC
OCEAN

0   100   500

Scale of Miles

World War II Allied Convoy

BATTLE IN THE
ARCTIC SEAS

THEODORE TAYLOR

STERLING

New York / London
www.sterlingpublishing.com/kids

A FLYING POINT PRESS BOOK

Design: PlutoMedia and John T. Perry III
Frontispiece: Getty Images
Front cover painting: Robert Bailey

STERLING and the distinctive Sterling logo are registered trademarks of
Sterling Publishing Co., Inc.

Library of Congress Cataloging in Publication Data

Taylor, Theodore, 1921–2006.
Battle in the arctic seas / Theodore Taylor.
p. cm. — (Sterling point books)
Originally published: New York : Crowell, c1976.
Includes bibliographical references and index.
ISBN-13: 978-1-4027-5123-3
ISBN-10: 1-4027-5123-0
1. World War, 1939–1945—Naval operations. 2. World War, 1939–1945—
Arctic Ocean. 3. Naval convoys—History—20th century. I. Title.
D771.T4 2007
940.54′29—dc22   2007012956

2   4   6   8   10   9   7   5   3   1

Published by Sterling Publishing Co., Inc.
387 Park Avenue South, New York, NY 10016
Original edition published by Thomas Y. Crowell Company
under the title *Battle in the Arctic Seas: The Story of Convoy PQ 17*
Copyright © 1976 by Theodore Taylor
New material in this updated edition
Copyright © 2007 by Flying Point Press
Maps copyright © by Richard Thompson, Creative Freelancers, Inc.
Distributed in Canada by Sterling Publishing
c/o Canadian Manda Group, 165 Dufferin Street
Toronto, Ontario, Canada M6K 3H6
Distributed in the United Kingdom by GMC Distribution Services
Castle Place, 166 High Street, Lewes, East Sussex, England BN7 IXU
Distributed in Australia by Capricorn Link (Australia) Pty. Ltd.
P.O. Box 704, Windsor, NSW 2756, Australia

Printed in China
All rights reserved

Sterling ISBN-13: 978-1-4027-5123-3
ISBN-10: 1-4027-5123-0

For information about custom editions, special sales, premium and corporate purchases,
please contact Sterling Special Sales Department at 800-805-5489 or
specialsales@sterlingpub.com.

To Howard E. Carraway
and a ship called Troubador

ACKNOWLEDGMENTS

The author cannot adequately express his gratitude to Howard E. Carraway for permission to include in this book portions of his previously unpublished diary. He kept the diary to help his wife, the late Avis Norman Carraway, to understand what the historic convoy was all about. Mr. Carraway also supplied me with copies of other documents, photographs, and sketches. Additionally, he provided invaluable advice.

I would also like to thank Ms. Anna C. Urband, Assistant Head, Magazines and Books, Office of Information, U.S. Navy Department, for her assistance and advice in researching the story. D. C. Allard, Operational Archives Branch, Naval History Division, extracted important information from the four-drawer file cabinet that holds material on the subject of PQ 17. The Jacksonville, Florida, Times-Union was extremely helpful in providing details of the sabotage of the Confidenza in that port in 1941.

CONTENTS

xi

CONTENTS

CHAPTER 1

THE GATHERING SHIPS

DOZENS OF CARGO SHIPS—THEIR DECKS STUDDED with Army tanks, crated military aircraft, and barrels of gasoline, their holds jammed to bursting with other implements of war—ride silently at anchorage in Iceland. It is the third week of June 1942. Soon the ships will sail in an Allied convoy. Destination: Russia.

Since early May, the bulky, slow-moving vessels have been gathering here at bleak Hvalfjördur anchorage, near Iceland's capital city of Reykjavik. Now they await a vast armada of British and American warships to escort them—convoy them—through the Arctic seas to the ports of Murmansk and Archangel in northern Russia.

Understandably, the seamen in the merchant ships are somewhat frightened. The run to Russia is perilous. German high-altitude bombers, dive bombers, torpedo planes, and U-boats are certain to attack.

Mixed with their fear is a certain resentment. Many sailors question the necessity of hauling supplies to the Soviet Union. No American or British troops are directly involved in Russia's desperate struggle against Germany. Why should the seamen risk their lives for the defense of a Communist nation? The answer is a simple one: Russia will collapse unless she receives ammunition, guns, tanks, and aircraft.

German troops have driven deep into the Soviet Union. They are now at the gates of the great cities of Leningrad and Stalingrad. Smolensk, Kharkov, Odessa, and Sevastopol have already fallen. The Germans are even encamped near Moscow.

Though the sailors at Hvalfjördur are not too concerned with Russia's problems, or, for that matter, with the history of the global conflict they are now engaged in, the facts about the war have a direct bearing on their convoy, PQ 17—a naval operation destined to be remembered for as long as there are ships on the sea.

World War II broke out almost three years earlier, in September 1939, when Germany, under the dictator Adolf Hitler, invaded Poland. A few days later England and France declared war on Germany. The following year Italy joined the fighting as Germany's ally. By then, Hitler's soldiers had conquered

Norway, Denmark, Belgium, the Netherlands, Luxembourg and, finally, France. In the summer of 1941 German divisions invaded Russia. Hitler had plans to dominate Europe, if not the world.

Several months later, on December 7, 1941, Japanese bombs exploded on the great United States naval base at Pearl Harbor, Hawaii. America, under President Franklin D. Roosevelt, formally entered what was now truly a world war.

In this third week of June 1942, gunfire sounds from the Soviet Union to the African deserts to such faraway Pacific islands as Wake and Guadalcanal. Pitted against the Axis powers of Germany, Italy, and Japan are the Allied nations— Great Britain, the United States, and Russia, along with a number of other countries.

In World War I, twenty-odd years previous, the Allies had learned that they must stand together or they would fall together. The consequences of a defeat of Russia now cannot even be considered. Hitler would not only control all of Europe but would obtain a gateway to the continent of Asia.

The Soviet Union must stand, and the ships of PQ 17 must sail without regard to danger.

At the moment, as indicated by the freighters swinging at anchor in Iceland, the single most important Allied war effort is supply. Many tons are needed to equip and feed just one platoon of soldiers, thousands of barrels of fuel oil to keep one naval ship in action, thousands of gallons of aviation gasoline for a single squadron of fighter planes.

More and more, the United States is the major source of military equipment for both Britain and Russia. Because of its great distance from Germany and Japan, America is not subject to the devastating air raids that have hit the big industrial cities of Great Britain and the Soviet Union, disrupting manufacturing. With abundant raw materials, American factories are working around the clock to provide war goods to all the Allied nations. Ultimately the supplies must be transported. Large ships are the only means to carry the cargoes overseas—aircraft are small and slow, and most do not have the range to fly the oceans.

In World War I, Germany almost defeated the Allies by choking off the sea lanes with submarine attacks. The German strategy has not basically changed. Allied cargo ships are being sunk all across the Atlantic, and in the Mediterranean and Caribbean Seas. This very week, along the east coast of America, thirteen merchant ships will be torpedoed by German submarines.

The merchant sailors at Hvalfjördur, civilians all, spend little time with thoughts of Hitler's grand military strategies. Nor are they occupied with the defensive tactics of the generals and admirals under President Roosevelt, Prime Minister

4

Winston Churchill of Great Britain, and Premier Josef Stalin of the Soviet Union. A number have already survived U-boat attacks in various parts of the world. They call themselves "torpedo bait." They have seen other ships blossom in flames. They have passed lifeboats and heard their fellow seamen crying for help, and have been unable to stop to pick them up. Even to slow down is to risk the blast of a torpedo—a "tinfish."

The civilian sailors receive high pay—including danger wages, or war bonuses—for manning these ships, which are often loaded with ammunition or high octane gasoline. Though they are not a very disciplined lot in comparison with military men, many have shown great courage against superior odds. Some freighters and tankers have sailed with no more armament than the captain's .45-caliber pistol.

As in World War I, the best protection against enemy attack is convoying—huddling the cargo ships together and providing warships as escorts. They move as a group to their destination.

The runs to Murmansk and Archangel in Russia are called "PQ" convoys, after a British naval officer, Commander P. Q. Edwards. The British Navy has the prime responsibility for routing and guarding the ships bound for Russia. For the return trip from the Soviet Union, the designation is changed to "QP."

* * *

In Hvalfjördur, the arrival drama is always the same. As the ships come in slowly and drop anchor, men appear on deck— some from galley spaces, others from the engine room. Standing quietly at midship rails or by the bitts on the fantail (the stern), they stare solemnly at Iceland's brown lava cliffs, where anti-aircraft guns point their snouts at the sky.

The bleak setting does not improve their spirits. The wind blows constantly across the Hvalfjördur roadstead, and the sky is usually gray. Seals swish about in the water. Seabirds— puffins, guillemots, kittiwakes, and Arctic skuas—twitter eerily.

In 1940 Great Britain occupied Iceland, to prevent the Germans from taking the island and to assure its availability as a possible key location in winning control of Arctic waters. The Allies also needed the snow-capped islands off Iceland as bases from which to make aerial reconnaissance of the northern seas. In 1941 the United States assumed military command of Iceland.

For six months now, the merchant sailors have been hearing fragments of stories about the convoys to Russia. Men have gone mad on the Murmansk run, they've been told. One convoy, PQ 13, was assaulted by teams of German planes and submarines; PQ 15 was under continuous attack for 48 hours. Since the convoys began last September, many ships have been lost.

The mariners have heard the tales in waterfront bars in port cities, and in hiring halls in Philadelphia, New York, and Boston, where union seamen report for assignment. Unfortunately many of the stories are true—and there is some visible evidence close at hand.

At this moment the rusty, battered SS *Carlton* swings at anchor in the roadstead. Loaded with Army tanks, tank ammunition, and other explosives, she had sailed in PQ 16 only a few weeks before. On May 25, with the ships under heavy air attack, bombs exploded near her hull, breaking steam and oil lines and opening seams in her ancient hull plates. She limped back to Iceland under tow by a trawler. On a previous run, ice had damaged her and she'd had to return then also. Now, having been hurriedly repaired, the *Carlton* is ready for a third try at reaching Murmansk.

The men eye her, wondering if she is a "Jonah"—a bad luck ship. Some have heard that the *Carlton*'s naval armed guard crew accidentally shot down a friendly plane during the PQ 16 action, which is an ill omen without question. Sailors can be very superstitious.

Beyond the threat of enemy action, the men fear the water itself, perhaps as much as bombs and torpedoes. It will be gray and flat this time of year, as smooth as fresh paint except where it is cobbled with ice. Yet even in summer it is so cold that no man can live in it for very long.

In summer and winter, there are violent snowstorms above the Arctic Circle. In winter no amount of clothing offers adequate protection. Lookouts come off watch with icicles on their noses and beards. Ice forms on the decks and pipes of the ships—on the bows and foredecks it is sometimes six feet thick.

Now, in summer, the weather won't be as harsh, but the ships will travel in almost constant daylight. This far north in late June the nights are less than two hours long. There will be little darkness in which to hide. The men pray for fog.

Indeed, the factor of constant daylight is very much on the minds of Admiralty planners in London. The winter convoys were hidden by the long Arctic night. But, as PQ 16, under attack for six straight days, has just discovered, summer convoys would be sleepless.

PQ 17 will sail north along the western coast of Iceland into Denmark Strait, then northeast to about latitude 75 degrees north, skirting the east coast of lonely Jan Mayen Island, between Greenland and German-occupied Norway. From there the ships will travel more or less due east until they pass Bear Island and Spitsbergen; then southeast into the Barents Sea, and finally south to Murmansk or to the mouth of Russia's White Sea for entry into the port of Archangel.

Even the names of the places are cold, lonely, uninviting. Yet hopeful rumors circulate around the ships.

"The convoy won't sail until the fog comes in."

"The Limeys [the British], by God, are going to provide three aircraft carriers to get us through."

"The convoy will be canceled because of the losses suffered by PQ 16."

Not one of these rumors has any truth in it.

CHAPTER 2

A SHIP CALLED *TROUBADOR*

A YOUNG NAVAL OFFICER, PLEASANT-FACED, SLENDER and sandy-haired, moves about the cluttered deck of an old merchant ship in the anchorage. Newly commissioned as an ensign—the lowest officer rank in the U.S. Navy—Howard Carraway, twenty-four years old, is commander of the armed guard crew of the SS *Troubador*.

Defensive guns, manned by naval personnel, are aboard each cargo ship. During enemy action in convoy, they augment the guns of the escorting warships. If the merchant vessels travel singly, as they often do in coastal waters, the armed guard crews are their sole defenders.

Since the arrival of the *Troubador* at Hvalfjördur in mid-May, Carraway has spent much time preparing his eight-man gunnery unit for the dash through Arctic seas. Gunnery drills are held daily. Carraway and his men also instruct volunteer members of the merchant crew in gunnery and ammunition supply.

Ensign Howard Carraway, U.S. Naval Reserve, is rather typical of the armed guard officers aboard the American merchant vessels of PQ 17. None are professional military men. The single gold stripe on their jacket sleeves is new and shiny bright.

Born in the sleepy rural village of Olanta, South Carolina, Carraway had never dreamed of joining the Navy—least of all of sailing to Russia. After graduating from college he became a reporter for, then managing editor of, a newspaper in Florence, another small South Carolina town.

The daily headlines in his paper told him that war was inevitable, and finally, in September 1941, he resigned his job to join the Navy. Commissioned little more than a month after the attack on Pearl Harbor, he married pretty Avis Norman and soon afterward reported to the bustling training base at Little Creek, Virginia. When he took the train to Philadelphia to present himself for duty aboard the *Troubador*, his bride returned home. Carraway, a peaceful, thoughtful young man, now finds himself gunnery boss of a slow, creaky, coal-burning merchantman.

During war, men are often picked for assignment by alphabetical order: "Abbott, Baker, Cohen, Dodds . . ." Most of

Carraway's enlisted men have been selected in just this manner. By pure happenstance, four of them are from Florida. A cross section of America, they are rated apprentice seamen. All but one are fresh from basic training, or "boot camp," and several weeks of gunnery instruction at Little Creek.

There is Tom Berry, aged eighteen, blond and sturdy. He plays the piano and wants to become a professional musician—if he can live through the war. Jesse Brannen, about the same age, is a farm boy and always the first to step forward when a volunteer is needed. Albert Busbin, freckled, quiet, not yet twenty, is already an expert mechanic. Bob Campbell, tall and bucktoothed, looks lazy and, in Carraway's opinion, is lazy. Charlie Wheatley is a smart, hard youth from Philadelphia, a physical fitness buff. Dick Harris, from Altoona, Pennsylvania, is a signalman; he has a tendency to become violently seasick. Bill Lawson, a Virginia farm boy, is a radio operator. The only professional in the gun crew is a petty officer—coxswain Maurice Wilds, from Indiana farm country. Wilds has served four years in the regular Navy and is almost as old as Carraway. Slightly built, sharp-featured, with tousled brown hair, Petty Officer Wilds knows what he is doing and how to do it. He functions as immediate gun crew boss under Carraway.

In all truth, the guns of the *Troubador* are not likely to panic the enemy. The 4-inch .50-caliber "cannon," mounted on a

13

platform at the stern, was built in World War I, more than twenty years ago. The "4.50," as it is known, with a barrel about the size of a telephone pole, cannot elevate higher than 45 degrees, which practically eliminates it for anti-aircraft work.

There are four .30-caliber Lewis machine guns—two in the steel tubs on either bridge wing, another pair by the sides of the after deckhouse over the crew's quarters. However, the *Troubador* is lucky: some ships have sailed in these waters without any guns. And the gun on one ship now in the road-stead was recently removed from Baltimore's City Park. America was not prepared for the sudden start of war, despite all the warnings.

The *Troubador* is certainly one of the most interesting ships in Hvalfjördur anchorage. All of her merchant officers are Norwegian and speak English with difficulty. Carraway sometimes has difficulty understanding them.

According to legend, the Norwegians' Viking ancestors were huge, bearded men, but Captain George Salvesen is a wizened, button-nosed runt. Barely five feet three inches tall, he might weigh 125 pounds after a full meal. However, the tiny master has spent his life at sea. He has the sharp, penetrating eyes of a veteran sailor. Speaking English with a heavy accent, he pronounces his "w's" as "v's," his "t's" as "d's," his "j's" as "y's."

The chief engineer, Ingebretsen, is as massive as Salvesen is small. In his seventies, the white-haired Ingebretsen is a pleasant but very profane man. Chief Mate Ericksen is also a veteran seaman. After sailing five years in the Orient, he had been bound for home and family in Norway when the Nazis occupied the country in April 1940. Ericksen hates the Germans.

Aside from Carraway and his gun crew, there are not many Americans on this ship. Fortunately for Carraway, pudgy "Sparks" Sauls, the vessel's merchant marine radio operator, is from Cades, South Carolina, only a few miles from Olanta. Carraway and Sparks often talk nostalgically about the Carolina low country—the Lynches and Pee Dee Rivers, and good old Florence County.

The ship's cook is a full-blooded American Indian named Bill Miller. There is a bearded intellectual from Philadelphia, Chester Dimmock, a combination steward and purser. Carraway and his gunners are friendly with Dimmock and Miller.

The majority of the other merchant seamen are foreign nationals, some of whom, because their countries have no immediate stake in it, couldn't care less who wins the war. Among the seventeen nationalities on board are crewmen from South Africa, Uruguay, Poland, Portugal, Spain, Belgium, Norway, Grand Cayman Island, England, Scotland, and Wales.

Prior to reporting to Captain Salvesen, Carraway had read

stories about tramp ships and their tough, unruly, polyglot crews. The stories had always seemed to him romantic and not particularly true to life, but the *Troubador* has changed Carraway's mind. Such ships do exist, and in the past few weeks he's begun to wonder how this polyglot crew will react when bombs start to fall.

Ships, like people, have distinct personalities. Some are happy; others are dark and brooding. Some are easy to handle; others are donkey stubborn. Some seem weak-willed while others are determined to survive against the odds of weather and sea—and even war. When a ship is launched, no one can predict her personality, or where she will go and what she will do. The *Troubador* has already had her share of trouble and intrigue.

In 1920, a freighter slid down the building ways of the Furness Shipbuilding Company into the choppy river Tees, at the port of Middlesbrough, England. Her name was SS *Ulisse*.

She was 412 feet in length, 55 feet in width, and 34 feet in depth, and her bow was reinforced for icebreaking because of the possibility that she would be used in northern waters. For the period, she was a good-looking vessel. Carrying a single stack in her ample midship section, she was composed of two separate structures. She had a classy "cruiser stern," copied after the medium-heavy warships of the day. Her interior was comfortable and in many areas wood-paneled. There was space for a few passengers.

With two cargo holds forward of the midship houses and two aft, the *Ulisse* was capable of carrying 6000 tons of cargo. An extra hold, known as a bunker, was used for her fuel, which was coal. Naked to the waist, stokers heaved the coal into the fireboxes beneath her boilers to manufacture steam for her turbine engines. Coal, not oil, was the principal fuel for most of the ships of the era.

The *Ulisse* roamed the Atlantic and Mediterranean for a few years and then was sold to a Belgian company, which rechristened her the SS *Robilante*. Soon thereafter an Italian company bought her and renamed her SS *Confidenza*. Under that name she steamed the oceans for almost fifteen years. In the meantime newer and faster ships were built, and by 1940, when Italy declared war on England and France, the *Confidenza* was down to hauling such lowly cargoes as scrap iron.

While in Jacksonville, Florida, to load cargo for a return voyage to Genoa, Italy, she was detained by the United States government. Although still neutral in 1940, America would not let her sail home to provide materials for Mussolini's war machine. So she sat in Jacksonville, rusting away, for almost a year. Then in March 1941, on orders from the Italian government, her crew sabotaged her, wrecking the engines.

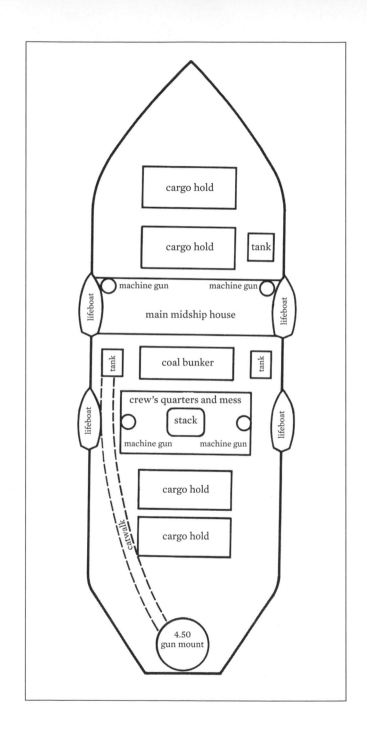

Promptly confiscated by the United States, the former *Confidenza* eventually went to a repair yard. There were plans to give her to England. The British certainly needed her. But the attack on Pearl Harbor abruptly changed those plans.

The new U.S. War Shipping Administration, an agency created to handle merchant ships and cargoes, registered her as a Panamanian vessel. (Ships of one country are often registered in another for tax reasons or to avoid having to assign higher-paid union crews to them. It was for this latter reason that the old freighter flew the flag of the Republic of Panama, though she was under direct control of the United States government.)

Her new name was *Troubador*.

In construction, Captain Salvesen's "rust bucket" is a very simple ship. Next to Carraway's cramped compartment in the main midship house, on the deck level, are spaces for his gunners. The officers' dining saloon and quarters for the engineering officers and the third mate are also on this level.

Directly above, on the boat deck level, are the quarters for the captain, second mate, and chief mate. The next level, the bridge deck, contains the wheelhouse, chartroom, radio shack and quarters for the radio operator. The bridge wings, narrow decks for observation, extend out on either side. Above all this is the flying bridge, the highest deck on the ship.

Separated from the main midship house by No. 3 hatch (the coal bunker) is still another deck structure. From it the stack emerges. In this three-level structure are the ship's galley and the crew's mess and quarters.

Four lifeboats hang from davits, two on each side of the ship, all located in the midships area very near the steel gun tubs, which are welded into place above the crew's quarters and on each bridge wing. The anti-aircraft guns can be manned instantly.

The *Troubador*'s chipped and battered deck is now a maze of cargo. Three M-3 General Grant medium tanks of twenty tons each, destined for the Russian army, are bolted down. Hundreds of barrels of ethylene gas are wedged in every available space not covered by massive crates. Along the port side a wooden catwalk has been constructed over the cargo to enable gunners to dash back to the 4.50. It will not be long before Carraway and his men have to sprint for the old "cannon" that pokes up from the steel platform above the *Troubador*'s cruiser stern.

CHAPTER 3
THE *TIRPITZ*

AS THE MEN OF PQ 17 GO ABOUT THEIR ROUTINE chores, the German Navy is formulating a plan to send a 42,000-ton Nazi battleship, the *Tirpitz*, into action against the convoy. At the moment, the massive man o' war is hidden in a fjord—an inland water passageway—in occupied Norway, near Trondheim.

The largest battleship in the world, the newly built *Tirpitz* has yet to fight her first sea battle, but she is capable of throwing nearly seven tons of steel across twenty miles of ocean from her main battery of eight 15-inch guns—seven tons every thirty seconds.

Smaller-bore batteries number thirty-four, and there are forty anti-aircraft tubs aboard her, each containing the latest German ack-ack gun. Six tubes can fire 20-inch torpedoes, and four small, short-ranged reconnaissance, or recco, planes can spy out the long columns of Allied ships. The huge dreadnought's flank (best) speed is 31 knots, enough to pace the fastest ship in any navy.

Yet the *Tirpitz,* pride of the German Navy, has been withheld from action for a number of reasons. Battleships need escorting destroyers, and destroyers are in short supply. Battleships are also vulnerable to air attack, and the Germans fear that the *Tirpitz* will be lost unless conditions are ideal. The great ship is the subject of much debate within the German Navy and she cannot put to sea without the express approval of Adolf Hitler.

On December 29, 1941, Grand Admiral Erich Raeder, commander in chief of the German Navy, conferred with Hitler about the possibility of sending the *Tirpitz* north from her German home base at the port of Wilhelmshaven. Raeder pointed out that the powerful ship would bolster the defense of Norway simply by her presence. She might also be used to attack the Russian-bound convoys.

Raeder guaranteed that moving the battleship to Norway would force the British to guard an even greater expanse of water—from the Faeroe Islands, north of Scotland, deep into the Barents Sea, in the Arctic. The *Tirpitz* would pose a continuous threat, even if she remained in port. She would keep the Allies off balance because they knew she was capable of steaming out on short notice.

Once on the open ocean, the *Tirpitz* could ride into the middle of a convoy and stop almost any merchant ship with a single shell. Or she could stand off and punch holes in the escort vessels while their own shorter-ranged guns remained silent, unable to touch her.

She was a terrible threat to the Allies, Raeder said.

Hitler finally agreed to the plan, though he remained fearful that the battleship would be lost in transit. Such a loss would be a devastating blow to German morale, military and civilian.

Raeder immediately ordered the *Tirpitz* readied for the dash to Norway, and she sailed from her berth at Wilhelmshaven on January 15, 1942. Her absence from German waters was noted by the British Admiralty on January 17. Reports from Allied spies in Germany were soon confirmed by aerial reconnaissance. The *Tirpitz* had fled.

On January 23, in a brief period of good weather, British Royal Air Force (RAF) recco planes located her at anchor at Asafjord, a sleepy Norwegian village near Trondheim. She was already camouflaged and tucked behind anti-torpedo netting to protect her from attack by Allied subs or torpedo boats.

Churchill reacted quickly on January 25 with a memo to his Chiefs of Staff Committee:

The destruction or even crippling of this ship is the greatest event at sea at the present moment. No other target is comparable to it. If she were even crippled it would be difficult to take her back to Germany. The entire naval situation throughout the world would be altered and the Naval command in the Pacific would be regained. The whole strategy of the war turns at this period on this ship, which is holding four times the number of British ships paralyzed, to say nothing of the two new American battleships retained in the Atlantic.

There is no question that the threat of the *Tirpitz* is forcing both the British and American Navies to keep a vast number of heavy ships on guard in the North Atlantic, thereby preventing their use for the war in the Pacific. It is estimated that as many as forty Allied warships, including battleships, aircraft carriers, and escorts, must be held in readiness in case the *Tirpitz* ventures out. A considerable number of aircraft are also kept at base, poised in readiness to attack.

She has already ventured out once. On the night of March 5, 1942, the German high command ordered an attack on convoy PQ 13, bound for Murmansk.

The *Tirpitz* sought "13" for two days, groping around in dense fog off the Norwegian coast. Although she did not locate the convoy, and came under brief attack by aircraft from the

British carrier *Victorious,* her presence thoroughly rattled Britain's naval chief, First Sea Lord Sir Dudley Pound.

As of this June week, the *Tirpitz* remains the most feared vessel on any sea. She has figured in many high-level discussions as pressures have mounted to steam cargoes toward Russia.

On April 27, President Roosevelt, needled rather constantly by Premier Stalin to provide more aid to the besieged Soviet armies, cabled Prime Minister Churchill to urge that the "ships begin moving." On the 30th, Roosevelt wrote to Churchill to inform him that between that date and June 1, a total of 107 American merchantmen would be loaded for departure to Russia; that the most important task he could envision would be to make positively certain that they sailed. He was implying that Russia could well collapse unless she was resupplied.

Stalin then wrote to Churchill:

I have a request for you. Some ninety steamers with various important war materiel for the USSR are bottled up at present in Iceland or in the approaches from America to Iceland. I feel it is incumbent on me to approach you with the request to take all possible measures to ensure the arrival of the above-mentioned in the USSR in the course of May, as this is extremely urgent for our front.

Some of these ships are still at Hvalfjördur. They are not bottled up by enemy action. They are simply caught in the slowness of organizing a giant convoy.

Churchill's reply, in part, was:

On account of Tirpitz, *and other enemy surface ships at Trondheim, the passage of every convoy has become a serious fleet operation. We are throwing all available resources into the solution of this problem, have dangerously weakened our Atlantic convoy escorts for this purpose, and as you are no doubt aware, have suffered severely. [Churchill is referring to the recent losses in the Soviet-bound convoys.]*

Even earlier, an alarmed Admiral Pound had warned Churchill's defense cabinet that losses might reach the point where the Arctic convoys would not be economical. Then Admiral Sir Jack Tovey, commander of the Home Fleet, who had the fighting responsibility, had advocated reducing the size of the convoys. The winter ice pack had not retreated sufficiently far westward to allow the ships to remain out of range of German bombers based in Norway.

However, against the political weight of Churchill, Roosevelt, and Stalin, sound naval judgment has been pushed aside. Churchill summed it up on May 17 in a memo to his military committee:

Not only Premier Stalin but President Roosevelt will object very much to our desisting from running the convoys now. The Russians are in heavy action and will expect us to run the risk and pay the price entailed for our contribution. The United States ships are queueing up. My own feeling, mixed with much anxiety, is that the convoy [PQ 16] ought to sail tomorrow. The operation is justified if only a half gets through.

"Only a half gets through"? Such was the desperation to resupply the Soviet Union. A shudder, if not pandemonium, would have cut across every ship bound for Russia had Churchill's statement been known to the men aboard them.

The following day, Admiral Pound wrote to his opposite in the American Navy, Fleet Admiral Ernest J. King:

These Russian convoys are becoming a regular millstone around our necks, and cause a steady attrition in both cruisers and destroyers.

The First Sea Lord has yet to feel the full weight of the millstone.

CHAPTER 4

THE CITADEL

TO THE MEN IN HVALFJÖRDUR ANCHORAGE, LONDON seems terribly distant. Even more remote is the notion that they are being given considerable attention in an underground fort in the British capital.

Extending from Westminster Hall to Trafalgar Square, Whitehall is one of the main thoroughfares of London. Bordering on it is the British Foreign Office, and leading off it is Downing Street, where Mr. Churchill lives. Also on Whitehall stands the British Admiralty.

For the most part, the European naval war is being waged from this collection of historic buildings. There is no busier place in all London than the Admiralty, from which Churchill's garden can be plainly seen.

What cannot be seen is a super-secret place called the

Citadel. Buried near the Admiralty, beneath the old Horse Guards Parade Ground, the Citadel is protected from Nazi bombs by tons of steel and concrete. In fact, it is probably a safer place than Churchill's own air raid shelter. A direct hit on the Parade Ground would do no more than jar it. This underground cellar fort houses the Admiralty's Operational Intelligence Centre. Down here there is no day or night. Lights are never turned out. Teleprinters—automatic typewriters— chatter incessantly, clacking out messages from around the world. Phones jangle. The movements of the men and women who work here are brisk and purposeful.

It is the very heart, the central control, of the eastern Atlantic sea war, and its visitors often include First Sea Lord Sir Dudley Pound and members of his staff. Even Churchill has been in the Citadel on occasion, to look over naval situations and ask pointed questions, chomping on his ever-present cigar.

One room contains the central plot, a vast chart of the Atlantic Ocean laid out on a large table. Hour by hour, sometimes minute by minute, Allied operations as well as known enemy operations are recorded on this plot by markers, flags, and lines. Convoys can be seen on it, progressing on their routes. Enemy U-boats can also be identified by the expert eye as to last known position. The plot constantly changes. Smaller plots fill in information on other areas of the world.

The central plot, fed by data from countless sources, reflects the progress of the sea war. In these months of 1942 the intricate business of convoying ships occupies the most attention.

Various methods are used to track enemy submarine, surface, and air units. For example, messages come from agents in Germany, Italy, and occupied countries such as Norway. They inform Allied contacts that a ship is about to sail, a submarine pack is readying to leave, or a squadron of aircraft are being shifted to a certain field. Aerial reconnaissance is another method.

A third method, one of the best, is used to keep tabs on U-boats, for instance. It is called HF/DF (high-frequency direction finding). In the American Navy, it is sometimes called "Huff-Duff." Experts monitor radio communications from enemy submarines or ships to obtain fixes on them, enabling central plot to position the unit.

It may seem impossible that a monitor can pick out of the air a particular signal and precisely identify its source. Yet each radio or wireless operator taps out messages in a definite pattern. The pattern is called his "fist." Monitors soon learn to recognize the fist of an operator. If U-boat 699, for instance, communicates to the German submarine command on shore, the monitor can almost immediately identify the pattern and thus the sub from which the message comes. The fix is

31

obtained by taking radio bearings on the signal. Time and time again the fix has proved to be amazingly accurate.

So at every hour of the day and night, at stations spotted around the world, monitors listen for communications from the enemy. Of course it works the other way around too. Germany also monitors Allied communications, and each side has broken certain of the other's codes, or ciphers. In this cold game of intelligence, each side knows much, though not all, of what the other is doing.

For instance, Germany is not fooled right now by the radio silence from Iceland. The Germans have made an estimate that a convoy is gathering and that it will soon sail. The silence itself indicates the strong possibility of this. German agents in Reykjavik have also passed on information that PQ 17 is getting ready to depart.

On the Allied side, there is one officer in particular who considers daily the possibility that the *Tirpitz* will go into action. His name is Norman Denning. His rank in the British Navy is Paymaster-Commander. His primary responsibility is to keep watch on German surface ships, and to predict what they will do and when.

Denning joined the Naval Intelligence Division in 1937, before the Citadel even existed. His accountant's training serves him well in his work.

In his basement office Denning keeps day-by-day track of Nazi surface ships, from battleships and cruisers to minesweepers and even armed merchant raiders—warships disguised as peaceful freighters.

If anyone in all the Allied navies is an expert on what moves such ships will make, it is Commander Denning. He is completely dedicated to his job. On more than one occasion the balding, bespectacled officer, pale from so many weeks underground, has slept on a bunk in his plot room. Sometimes he does not see the upper world for days.

Since her move to Trondheim in January, Denning has worried constantly about the *Tirpitz,* but he hasn't the slightest notion of the Germans' latest plans for the battleship. The operation they have designed, coded *"Rosselsprung"* (which means in English "Knight's Move" or "Knight's Gambit"), will involve not only the *Tirpitz* but submarines and aircraft as well. The purpose is to destroy PQ 17 totally. Grand Admiral Raeder has used the word "annihilate" in discussing the attack.

On June 15, Raeder was at Hitler's summer home, Berchtesgaden, to outline the operation. Raeder used a large chart to detail the favorable factors. Constant daylight is one. The position of the ice fields is another. The heavy floes to the west would force the convoy to travel on a course 200 to 250 miles from the Norwegian airfields—within easy bombing range.

The *Tirpitz,* he claimed, has every chance of steaming into the very center of PQ 17, sinking ships with every salvo.

Hitler listened and has agreed to Knight's Move, provided that any British or American aircraft carriers in the vicinity of the convoy be put out of commission before the *Tirpitz* carries out her raid. Otherwise the Allied carriers will be able to steam within 200 miles of the battleship and launch planes to sink this very valuable hull.

Pleased with himself, Raeder left Berchtesgaden, and full preparations for the attack were begun. Five days have passed and the plan is now being implemented.

The operational, or immediate, control will be in the hands of Admiral Rolf Carls, commander of Naval Group North, which is based at Kiel, a German port on the edge of the Baltic Sea. Carls has a mustache not unlike Hitler's plus an old-fashioned goatee. He is a very precise, dogged man.

The tactical, or fighting, command will rest with General Admiral Otto Schneiwind, aboard the *Tirpitz.* Balding, gaunt-faced, thin-lipped, Schneiwind is sometimes called "the Undertaker" by German sailors—behind his back, of course. He does resemble in appearance a movie version of a funeral parlor attendant. He is, however, tough and cocky.

The U-boats will be operated by Admiral Hubert Schmundt, Admiral Nordmeer, or commanding admiral of the

Arctic. Aircraft of Luftflotte V, the German 5th Air Command, will be led by Colonel General Hans-Jurgen Stumpff.

Admiral Schmundt has already ordered three of his white-painted Ice Devil subs to stand by for immediate departure. Their orders are to proceed to the likely route of convoy PQ 17 and lie in wait. Operation Knight's Move is under way.

CHAPTER 5

THE CHESS MOVES BEGIN

AROUND NOON ON JUNE 23 A CONVOY PULLS INTO Hvalfjördur anchorage, bringing the last of the Allied ships that will make the run to Russia. There are now thirty-five destined to deliver cargoes at either Murmansk or Archangel. Twenty-two fly the United States flag. Some are new Liberty ships—bulky vessels built by bookkeepers or housewives miraculously turned welders. Others are sluggish Hog Island types, born in World War I, or ships of distinctive company design, such as the Matson Lines' *Olopana*.

The British have their usual flock of dun-colored Empire freighters on hand. One, the *Empire Tide*, carries a single Hurricane fighter plane to be catapulted from her deck during action. The aircraft cannot be recovered. The pilot will have to crash-land in the icy sea and hope to be picked up.

The Dutch have contributed the *Paulus Potter*. Two Russian tankers, the *Azerbaijan* and the *Donbass,* are now riding from hook not far away.

The older hulls in the roadstead are viewed with misgiving. Convoy speed is always set at the best possible speed of the slowest ship. With the awkward, creaking Hog Islanders, that means something less than a steady 10 knots, hardly a safe speed for the waters off Norway.

Ensign Carraway spends the day checking out all the anti-aircraft guns once again and sends his crew through a gas mask drill. The Germans have not used poisonous gas in this war but Carraway wants to be prepared. The gas masks can also be used in heavy smoke should the ship catch fire. Finally, he tells Petty Officer Wilds that he thinks they are ready to go except for a supply of tracer ammunition—bullets that glow, enabling the gunner to shoot with better accuracy.

Where ammunition is concerned, Carraway is becoming gluttonous. He is operating on the single-minded principle of the more, the better. Earlier he persuaded the supply ship USS *Melville* to part with 6000 rounds for the Lewis machine guns and has vigorously complained because he is short of tracers. The young officer who once described himself as "the Great American Chicken"—meaning that he did not want to fight anyone—a dedicated "dove" whose most violent activity was fishing, is slowly being converted into a confirmed "hawk."

Something else bothers Carraway these days: the three Army tanks on the *Troubador*'s deck. One is forward of the midship house; the other two are located outboard of the hatch to the coal bunker, just outside the ensign's porthole. Each has a beautiful new .37-millimeter gun projecting from its turret. Elevated, the long barrels could pound away at aircraft, using tracers boxed down in the cargo holds.

Such a shame to have those lovely guns, daubed with preservative grease and a plastic coating called "ackumpunkie," sitting idly, he thinks. Yet no one is supposed to touch them until their arrival in Murmansk. Only under dire emergency can cargo be entered or used. The offense, known as barratry, is punishable by a prison term.

However, the .37-mm's continue to tempt Carraway. He finds it difficult not to look at them each time he steps out on deck. He discusses the tank guns with Maurice Wilds. The petty officer, being of the same mind, declares he would love to pop a few rounds from them, simply to see how they work. The Russians wouldn't mind—or would they?

The only notable event in Hvalfjördur on Friday, June 26, is the discovery of a woman aboard the *Azerbaijan,* the big Russian tanker. Then another is seen! The news is blinkered from bridge to bridge by Navy signalmen. Binoculars become a premium item on any ship near the *Azerbaijan* as crew members line up to take a look.

By dinner hour, there are jokes going around that the *Azerbaijan*'s chief mate is not only female but pregnant. She'll have her baby on the sea road to Murmansk while the German Luftwaffe (Air Force) sings a cradle song from on high. Laughter *is* needed at Hvalfjördur.

In fact, there are more than a dozen women aboard the Soviet ships. They work in the steward's department, preparing and serving food and cleaning the officers' quarters. They also act as gunners. What's more, they have a reputation as expert shots.

On this same day, hundreds of miles away, leaves have been canceled at all the Norwegian naval bases of the German northern command. Similarly, leaves have been canceled at the Luftwaffe bases at Bardufoss, Banak, Petsamo, and Kirkenes. Colonel General Stumpff has issued orders to keep 200 planes in readiness around the clock, once PQ 17 is sighted. The cradle songs will be noisy.

But the Germans are not alone in preparation for the departure of this convoy. At Scapa Flow, the anchorage of the British fleet off Pomona Highlands, at the northern end of Scotland, a force of heavy ships is making up.

Under the command of Admiral Sir Jack Tovey—the same

officer who tried to trap the *Tirpitz* in March—who will be flying his flag on the battleship *Duke of York,* it will include the American battleship *Washington,* the British aircraft carrier *Victorious,* three cruisers, and a baker's dozen of destroyers and corvettes.

Tovey's ships will stay far away from the convoy, out of range of German shore-based bombers, unless there are signs that the *Tirpitz* is closing in on PQ 17. Then Tovey will steam his fleet full speed toward the German dreadnought. At least, those are the plans.

At Seydisfjördur, an anchorage on the other side of Iceland, the British close escort—including two anti-aircraft ships bristling with guns and three rescue vessels to seine men from icy waters—has collected. The rescue vessels, *Rathlin, Zaafaran,* and *Zamalek,* all small merchantmen, are specially equipped for lifesaving. Each has a small hospital and medical staff aboard.

Also nested deep in the long wedge of anchorage that invades the high mountains around Seydisfjördur is a flotilla of British destroyers, as well as corvettes (which are small destroyer-type ships), minesweepers, and armed trawlers. The low-lying hulls of two British submarines are visible. They will accompany the convoy, too, ready to submerge and take a torpedo shot at the *Tirpitz* should they spot her.

If this seems to be already adequate protection, there is still another group at Seydisfjördur: a cruiser task force under the command of British Rear Admiral Louis H. K. ("Turtle") Hamilton. In this task force, in addition to a pair of His Majesty's ships, the *London* and the *Norfolk,* will be the American cruisers *Wichita* and *Tuscaloosa,* now anchored at Hvalfjördur. To screen these large ships are assigned a number of British destroyers and corvettes, plus the American destroyers *Wainwright* and *Rowan.* While Tovey will stay several hundred miles away with his carrier and pair of battleships, Admiral Hamilton's ships will provide closer-range support of the convoy.

In total, this is a staggering assembly of warships to make certain that a motley group of merchantmen arrive safely in Russia. It is testimony both to the power of the *Tirpitz* and to the fact that PQ 17 does contain 188,000 tons of military supplies for Stalin's beleaguered armies.

There are rumors at Seydisfjördur, too. They specifically center on the German battleship. In some of the men o' war there is hope that she'll come out and swap shells. Among those of such a mind, PQ 17 is seen as bait to lure the *Tirpitz* away from Trondheim.

As of this moment, eight British, one Free French, and two Russian submarines are already moving toward patrol lines in the seas off Norway to keep an eye open for German surface forces.

The chess moves have begun on both sides.

CHAPTER 6

CONFERENCES

PQ 17 WILL SAIL TODAY, SATURDAY, JUNE 27, 1942. At 9 A.M., launches bob at gangways or rope ladders of all the ships. Rain pelts the gray water, and the air is chill. From every point of view, it is a miserable day.

Crewmen watch as the captains of the merchantmen descend into the boats and are whisked off to attend the commodore's conference aboard the SS *River Afton,* a British freighter. The *River Afton,* a relatively new ship, berths Commodore J. C. K. Dowding, Royal Navy Reserve, and his small staff, made up mostly of signalmen.

While the escort commander, a senior officer aboard one of the close escort warships, is in direct control of the convoy, the commodore is senior officer of the merchant ships. He urges the ships to "keep station"—to stay in their positions at a steady speed—and chastises them when they make too much oily smoke, which enables enemy aircraft or submarines to spot them. He also makes other decisions concerning safety and cargo, staying in close visual or radio contact with the escort commander. Most convoy commodores are either high-ranking retired naval officers or very senior merchant captains.

A compact man of sixty-one, Commodore Dowding has been sailing in various types of ships for forty years, and for the past twenty years he's been a ship's master. In 1940 he was one of those who went to the beaches of Dunkirk to rescue stranded British soldiers. Dowding is a pleasant man with an engaging smile.

As he speaks, the commodore assumes that every master present has sailed in one or more convoys. First he describes the composition of PQ 17: the ships are to travel four deep in nine columns. Then he reads off the proposed route and prescribed speeds. He says that the close escort, now at Seydisfjördur, will join the convoy at sea July 1. Locally based small ships will escort it until then. Dowding discusses communication procedures and the successive rallying points should the convoy be scattered. He also calls attention to the rescue ships that will be immediately behind the convoy, to scoop survivors out of the water if a ship is bombed or torpedoed.

Dowding, talking quietly in the soft-lit wardroom, ends the conference by distributing an envelope of instructions to each captain. The envelopes contain secret communication codes and are not to be opened until the hour of departure.

Back aboard his ship, each captain informs his chief mate and chief engineer that the convoy will definitely leave Hvalfjördur at 5 P.M. Most of the ships have been preparing since dawn, building up steam in the boilers.

Meanwhile, Ensign Carraway has had varied fortune aboard the USS *Melville,* where he has gone to try to get more ammunition for his *Troubador.* They cannot supply him with tracer bullets, but the *Melville's* executive officer shows Carraway a dispatch from Naval Operations in Washington. The teletyped slip of paper grants permission to "broach cargo"— to enter it—for defense of the ships. So the tank guns *can* be utilized! Carraway is delighted.

Rain is still falling when, at 1 P.M., the merchant masters reassemble in the large YMCA hall at Hvalfjördur for the main convoy conference. This time, the room is full of gold braid. Several admirals are present, including Rear Admiral Hamilton, commander of the First Cruiser Squadron. Also in attendance is Commander John E. ("Jack") Broome, the escort commander, in charge of the close escort force. Broome is a well-liked figure in the British Navy, a man with a hearty laugh and winning sense of humor.

Commodore Dowding speaks first, very briefly. Then Broome rises to assure all the merchant captains that he will do his best to provide protection. Finally, Rear Admiral Hamilton addresses the group of nearly 200 men. He explains the vast support being given to PQ 17—the close escort; his own cruiser force; Tovey's distant force of battleships and an aircraft carrier.

The RAF (Royal Air Force), says "Turtle" Hamilton, will bomb the German airfields in Norway in an attempt to neutralize them. Allied submarines will operate to contain German surface forces. Wisely, Hamilton does not mention the threat of the *Tirpitz*. Listening to him, though, some of the merchant masters uneasily speculate about why such massive forces are necessary to protect only thirty-five ships. Few of them realize that their operation comprises, in total, more than sixty ships with almost 25,000 men in them. The cargo in the freighters alone, including 4,246 vehicles and 297 aircraft, is valued at more than $700 million.

The captains return to their ships and prepare to sail. It is time to test engines and to rotate the bridge telegraph, its bell sound communicating to engineers below that departure is imminent. Soon there are whistles bleating all across the roadstead, some hoarse, some mournful. The serenade is a fitting farewell to bleak Hvalfjördur anchorage.

Pennants that identify each ship by number break out from bridge halyards. Men with hoses squirt water down the hawse pipes to wash mud from the clanking anchor chains. The ship's captains, now heavily clothed for long, cold hours on the bridge, stare toward the foredecks as the chief mates supervise the heaving in of the anchors.

By 5 P.M. the *Troubador*'s anchor is up, and the old ship begins to gather speed.

The story is much the same on each vessel. The log of the new American Liberty ship *Samuel Chase* reads:

1640 [4:40 P.M.], began weighing anchor
1655 [4:55 P.M.], engine slow ahead
1700 [5:00], anchor home, steaming in company with other
  ships of convoy
1810 [6:10], took departure of Reykjavik harbor, Iceland

Ensign Carraway makes an entry in his diary, which is written in the form of letters to his wife.

We are under way for Russia. Weighed anchor in Hvalfjördur and passed the boom through the great anti-

submarine nets. We are out of Reykjavik harbor and into deep water. Steam up. Dander up. Thumbs up. The gallant warrior, the Joan d'Arc of the Battle of the Atlantic, the stepchild of misfortune and Father Time, our dearly beloved and frequently cursed tub, the Troubador, *is now under way again, headed for what, I wonder? For a humdrum voyage? Or for disaster?*

CHAPTER 7

ICEBERGS

IN THE GROWING MURK, COMMODORE DOWDING orders the ships to form into two columns about five miles off Reykjavik. There is no breeze. The water is flat; the temperature is in the mid-forties.

On the bridge of the *Troubador*, Captain Salvesen, the collar of his heavy red hunting jacket high around his neck, says to Ensign Carraway in his thick Norse accent, "My back hurts. Ve're on de road to Roossia an' my back hurts already." A fat rope of charcoal smoke is uncoiling from the stack of the *Troubador*, and the tiny captain curses beneath his breath, shakes his head and goes into the bridgehouse to ring Chief Ingebretsen and complain. It will happen many times.

Carraway looks around at the other ships. They all ride low in the water. The *Alcoa Ranger,* out of Philadelphia, has 7,000 tons of steel and armor plate in her holds, nineteen tanks lashed to her deck. The *Peter Kerr* has tanks and aircraft on her deck and thousands of general cargo items crammed below. The British *Earlston* is transporting field guns for the Russian army as well as tons of ammunition. Crated Hurricane fighter planes are on her foredeck, drums of aviation gasoline on her afterdeck. All the ships are carrying more cargo than would be allowed in peacetime.

Soon the vessels, in two long columns, turn up their propellers to gain 7 knots—less than 10 miles an hour, a painfully slow speed. They settle down to station keeping, each ship guiding on the stern of the one ahead like elephants in a line.

In no time at all, PQ 17 registers its first casualty. The *Richard Bland*, an American ship, piles up on rocks that open a jagged hole in her plating. She will have to drop out and return to Hvalfjördur for repairs, then await another convoy.

As they reach a position off Cape Staalbjerghuk, Iceland, Commodore Dowding signals for the convoy to form into the prescribed nine columns, four ships to each column. After making certain that each ship knows of the new formation, he orders the "Execute" flag to be popped from the bridge halyard, then emphasizes it with a long blast from the *Afton*'s whistle.

The ships maneuver into position and, in the new

formation—one that Dowding hopes will last all the way to Russia—steam on toward Denmark Strait, the forbidding channel between Iceland and Greenland. Now about 600 yards apart in a stem-to-stern direction and about 1,000 yards port to starboard, the merchantmen ride in orderly columns. Speed is regulated so that more or less constant distances are maintained.

The *Troubador* is last in the second column on the port, or left, side. Her immediate neighbor to the left is the SS *William Hooper*. Directly ahead is the Britisher SS *Bolton Castle*. To starboard, or the right, is the Russian tanker *Donbass*. Behind the *Donbass,* to everyone's delight, is the rescue ship *Rathlin*.

The routine of convoying sets in. Deck officers eye their neighbors, hoping they'll maintain course and speed and won't smoke too much. At this hour, PQ 17 is a very ordinary convoy.

Shortly after 9 P.M., when the joke of night is on them, pale twilight appears far to the north, above the fog. Then the sky is briefly lit by the rays of the Aurora Borealis. At ten the sun rises again, its red light flickering across the caps of Iceland's glacier fields and reflecting from the sides of rugged black cliffs that reach into the ocean.

Allied patrol planes from the Keflavik base are still droning on the outer edges of the convoy, searching for lines of froth that might mean "U-boat." In view from the *Troubador* bridge

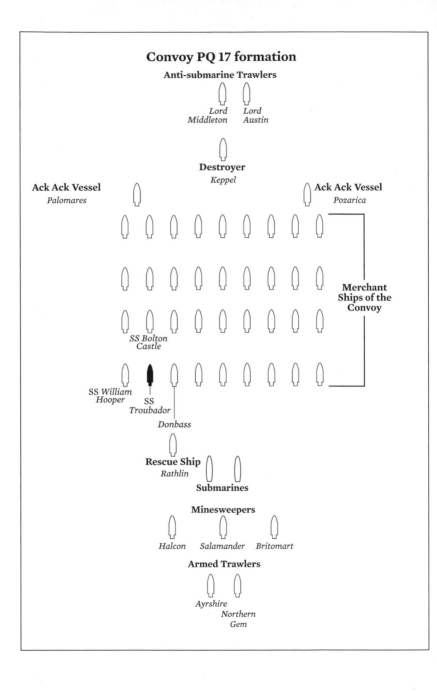

Convoy PQ 17 formation

Anti-submarine Trawlers

Lord Middleton *Lord Austin*

Destroyer
Keppel

Ack Ack Vessel
Palomares

Ack Ack Vessel
Pozarica

Merchant Ships of the Convoy

SS Bolton Castle

SS William Hooper SS *Troubador* *Donbass*

Rescue Ship
Rathlin

Submarines

Minesweepers

Halcon *Salamander* *Britomart*

Armed Trawlers

Ayrshire *Northern Gem*

are the small escort vessels, chugging along at angles that make them appear to be moving feelers of the columns.

It is bedtime for Ensign Carraway.

As Dowding turns the convoy into Denmark Strait, on June 28, with a steamy blast of the *River Afton*'s whistle, he breathes a sigh of relief. Patrol planes have spotted heavy fog ahead. Perhaps the ships can hide a little longer from the German recco planes that are certain to be snooping within a day or two.

By noon, floebergs—small icebergs—dot the water and pass gracefully between the lines of ships. By late afternoon they are no longer small, and they thud against the hulls.

Aboard the SS *Honomu*, Alan Harvie feels nervous. As he will recall later, "You could hear those things banging against us now and then. But it wasn't only the ice. If you came up on deck, there was this flat water and fog. Aside from the ship's noises and that whistle every thirty seconds, it was dead quiet. You could hardly see the ship in the next column over. It was spooky."

Ensign Carraway is too busy to think about the spooky sea. He has broken the seal on one of the Army tanks, the object of his attention for weeks. He finds that the .37-mm gun is in good shape. Next, with the aid of Chief Mate Ericksen, he enters a cargo hold to procure ammunition for the gun.

An hour later, the gun booms out nicely. Now training can begin for the men who will use it. The shell it fires is about fourteen inches long and weighs roughly ten pounds.

The day wears on, and then the weather lifts briefly. Carraway notes in his diary:

Our last sight of Iceland was typical: flat-topped, mesa-like mountains, jutting suddenly from the seas, wearing velvety white, lacy caps of clouds on their snow-covered peaks. They vanished into the fog an hour or so ago, almost at the same time we crossed the Arctic Circle and entered the famous, cold, ice-bound Norwegian Sea. I'm glad to have put Iceland behind us.

At about 3:30 the next morning Carraway is awakened by heavy pounding on the hull of the *Troubador*. He rouses from his bunk and goes out on deck. The ship is passing through a large ice field. Masses of brilliant white, blue, and green ice envelop the convoy. Around 5 A.M., with fog still shrouding the ships, and the visibility less than 50 yards, the convoy plows into even heavier ice. Almost immediately, the American *Exford* collides with a big floe, impaling it on her bow. Captain Ulrich signals Dowding that he's hit a berg, estimated to be 100 feet in width and at least 15 feet thick. The *Exford*'s bow has been crushed. Water flows into her forepeak, the empty space at the bow.

The British fleet oiler *Gray Ranger* and two other ships suffer ice damage too, but only the *Exford* is in danger of sinking. Commodore Dowding gives permission for her to return to port, and Captain Ulrich notes matter-of-factly in his logbook: "Vessel struck ice and forepeak stoved in. Returned. . . ."

The *Gray Ranger*, along to refuel the escort ships, is in no shape to make it to Murmansk either, and she will eventually trade places with the British tanker *Aldersdale*. Already PQ 17 is down to thirty-three ships, and the enemy hasn't even been sighted.

Ensign Carraway has little time to take note of the plight of the *Exford* and *Gray Ranger*. He has broken the seal on a second Army tank and now has a rather formidable battery of firepower on the *Troubador*. The tank turrets can be rotated to follow enemy aircraft, thumping tracer shells at them.

Also in the tanks are some submachine guns—handheld American "tommy" guns, also known as "Chicago pianos." Carraway has Maurice Wilds clean and prepare them. If the *Troubador* comes under attack, he will have volunteers fire them at the swooping Heinkels and Junkers, peppering away at the planes from the deck. The Chicago pianos are almost as effective as the Lewis guns.

Captain Salvesen remarks, with a chuckle, that his young American armed guard officer appears to be willing to throw "sticks, stones and tomato cans" at the Germans. That is quite true.

This same afternoon, 1,200 miles away at Scapa Flow, Admiral Sir Jack Tovey is preparing to take his force to sea from the heathland of Pomona. His course, with the battleships and the carrier *Victorious*, is toward Spitsbergen. There he will await a move by the *Tirpitz*.

In a last-minute phone conversation with the First Sea Lord in London, Tovey is shaken to learn that Admiral Pound has it in mind to scatter the convoy should the *Tirpitz* put to sea. The ships would break formation and run for Russian ports individually. The tactic has been used before with convoys, including earlier runs to Russia, but it leaves the merchant ships without protection. Even the slightest mention of a scattering operation dismays Tovey. He is very uneasy as the time approaches to weigh anchor from Scapa Flow.

CHAPTER 8

THE DIAMOND DEFENSE

SHORTLY BEFORE NOON ON TUESDAY, JUNE 30, the weather begins to clear, and at about three o'clock Commander Broome sights the plodding ships of PQ 17. Quickly he deploys his close escort around them. The little trawlers and minesweepers that have escorted the convoy this far signal "Good luck" as they chug off to return to Hvalfjördur.

Carraway watches the newly joined escort from the bridge wing of the *Troubador*. He counts a dozen ships and guesses that more are over the horizon. The antisubmarine trawlers *Lord Middleton* and *Lord Austin* are deployed ahead of the convoy, out of sight. Then the rest of the escort, led by Broome's destroyer *Keppel*, is arranged in a diamond formation that encloses the merchant ships. Riding just inside each outboard column are the ack-ack vessels *Palomares* and

Pozarica. Directly behind the convoy are the two submarines, P-614 and P-615, ready for the appearance of any Nazi surface units. At the after point of the diamond are the minesweepers *Halcyon, Salamander,* and *Britomart*, and in the far wake of the formation is another pair of armed trawlers, the *Ayrshire* and *Northern Gem*. A neat, orderly defense is now moving across the cold, quiet sea, screening the convoy from both air and sea attack.

The *Ayrshire* is definitely a ship to keep in mind. All the steel-hulled trawlers, each about 700 tons, look much alike with their single funnels, low well decks, and high bows. They are camouflaged blue and white to match the Arctic sea and ice. They were built for fishing in northern waters, not to fight wars. Yet, with their crews of reserve officers, fishermen, and tugboat men, they are serving admirably. The *Ayrshire* is typical of the rugged trawler fleet now fighting subs.

It is heartening for the men of the merchant ships to scan in every direction and see the firepower of the close escort and especially the bristling flak ships. Every conceivable type of usable gun, old and new, stands ready to face the enemy. There are such old reliables as Browning and Lewis machine guns, and newer and heavier anti-aircraft weapons like the Swedish Bofors and Oerlikons. There are launching arrays (called "pig troughs") for small rockets.

Some of the weapons don't really work too well—for

example, rockets that send into the air parachutes dragging cables, to entangle attacking planes. Some ships have the familiar barrage balloons that date back to World War I. Inflated, the balloons will float above the ships, dangling wires, to complicate enemy strafing runs.

Carraway stays on the bridge a while longer, enjoying the sight of the escort but bothered by the bitter cold. He is now wearing Arctic gear, topped by a heavy sheepskin coat, but despite all the clothing his teeth chatter and he shivers. It is almost zero degrees.

Off and on, until 4:30 A.M. the next day, July 1, Carraway returns to the bridge to take a look around. But the night of no darkness passes calmly and he finally goes to bed.

He would not sleep as soundly as he does if he knew what is taking place in Norway. Signaling from Naval Group North at Kiel, German Admiral Rolf Carls has ordered the *Tirpitz*, the heavy cruiser *Hipper*, and five other ships to prepare to leave Trondheim. They are to sail to Vestifjord, south of Norway's North Cape, where the *Tirpitz* will rendezvous with the pocket battleships *Scheer* and *Lützow*. Also at this hour of 6 A.M., ten German subs are lying in wait off Jan Mayen Island. They have not sighted PQ 17 as yet.

In the afternoon, as the convoy nears Jan Mayen, the tension mounts noticeably. The ships are now within range of Nazi aircraft based in Norway.

Carraway begins his diary for this date: "May flowers, April showers, June brides—but July?" He has awakened at 11:30 A.M. and, having had breakfast, is now on the bridge at thirty minutes past noon. There is visibility to each side of the convoy, but the ceiling is near zero—perhaps not more than 300 feet above the ships.

As the sound of airplane engines cuts suddenly through the blanket of fog, Carraway hops into the nearest gun tub, yelling at the second mate to ring the alarm. Although he can hear the aircraft, he cannot see it.

Then a destroyer on the starboard side of the convoy hurls heavy ack-ack fire blindly upward. The engine sounds fade away as the aircraft—likely a German reconnaissance plane— goes on its way untouched.

Carraway realizes that his heart is pounding, his hands unsteady on the Lewis gun. His first encounter with the enemy has been brief and harmless. However, the cat and mouse game off Jan Mayen Island has begun.

Shortly after two o'clock Commodore Dowding signals: "Stream fog buoys." The T-shaped markers flop overboard behind the stern of each ship. Helmsmen steer on the spurt of water raised by the buoy ahead. There are moments when, because of the fog, the stern of the preceding ship cannot be seen, and then the helmsman must rely solely on the knife of water to avoid collision.

The sea seems even more leaden than usual today, as smooth as oil paint. Overhead are thick, low clouds, which mingle with the dense surface fog. The weather conditions alone are nerve-wracking.

Then suddenly the visibility improves. Soon a lone aircraft approaches from the east, zooming into and out of the fog banks. "Action stations!"—the order to man all guns and prepare for possible battle—rings out across the ships. Sirens bleat on the escort vessels as they swing toward the target. On some of the merchant ships men begin spraying water across the decks to cut down the hazards of fire.

The plane is quickly identified as enemy: a German Focke-Wulff 200, a long-range maritime reconnaissance bomber. With four engines and the capability of staying aloft for many hours, the big recco craft is now content just to spy. It has found its prize and makes no attempt at a bombing run. The Focke-Wulff simply shadows PQ 17 for more than an hour while its crew calmly and carefully counts the merchant ships and their escort companions.

Then the pilot sends a report by wireless to his Norwegian base. It is routed to Admiral Carls at Kiel; to Raeder in Berlin; Schmundt at the Narvik, Norway, sub base; Schneiwind aboard the *Tirpitz;* and to Colonel General Stumpff of the Luftwaffe. Word sweeps across a dozen commands that the convoy has been located.

U-boats around Jan Mayen Island soon confirm the plane's observations. They have time for only a brief look at the mass of ships because Jack Broome's escort force is already beginning to toss depth charges at them. The sea slams and erupts.

On both sides it is a day of reconnaissance and messages, but the Allies are not as fortunate as the Germans. Because bad weather blankets Trondheim and the fjords, RAF recco planes cannot take pictures to verify that the *Tirpitz* is still at her mooring. There also is silence from the Norwegian agents. In the Citadel, Paymaster Commander Denning frets.

Furthermore, a disturbing message comes from Murmansk in the afternoon. The British senior officer there radios London that one third of the city has been destroyed by Nazi bombers. Many buildings are still burning. He advises that any ships coming to Murmansk may be total losses if there are further raids.

Though it is only 35 miles away from a German airfield in Norway, Murmansk has been the chief port of supply for the Soviet armies defending Moscow and Leningrad. It offers a year-round, ice-free approach through the Kola Inlet. But the docks, nestled beneath a series of hills, are constantly bombed by the Luftwaffe.

On the *River Afton*, Commodore Dowding's signal watch receives a copy of the Murmansk message. Dowding orders his navigation officer to prepare new courses that will lead all the ships into the White Sea and then to Archangel, at the mouth of Russia's Dvina River, instead of to Murmansk.

At dinner time, far away off Iceland, the crew of another Focke-Wulff makes an important sighting. The flyers soon notify the German 5th Air Command that they have spotted a heavy battle fleet. This is, of course, Admiral Tovey's distant force, cruising in a position to support PQ 17 as well as to prevent the breakout of the *Tirpitz* from Norway.

The German admirals are now aware of most of the chess pieces on the Allied strategy board. However, they do not know of Admiral "Turtle" Hamilton's cruisers playing hide and seek in the fog not far from Bear Island, northeast of PQ 17. Hamilton is hiding his ships purposely.

Meanwhile the convoy steams along under alert. Food loses its taste. Any sleep the men get is apt to be restless. They come out on deck to look at the sky and return inside to await the next clang of bells.

At about 10 P.M., Carraway, Wilds, and some of the armed guard crew test the second Army tank gun. "It works great. One more weapon to turn on the Germans," the ensign notes in his diary.

An hour later, Carraway is climbing toward the bridge for a cup of coffee—a pot of it bubbles continually in the bridge-house—when a lookout shouts, "Submarine on the port beam!" Carraway pounds up the ladder and notices that the third mate is standing stiffly on the wing, staring seaward, rather than hitting the alarm button. Carraway charges by him, sets the bell ringing, and then runs across the catwalk for the stern and the 4.50 gun.

Escort destroyers and corvettes are converging on the port quarter, coming in at an angle off the *Troubador*'s bow, heaving depth charges as they move along at top speed. The water mushrooms every two or three seconds and the *Troubador*'s hull shakes with each blast.

Carraway, Wilds, Charlie Wheatley, Campbell, Brannen, and Harris stay on the platform until the destroyers return to station. The ensign is disappointed by the merchant crew's reaction to this first serious threat. Only three of the civilian sailors have reported to their posts.

However, he knows that he can count on Bill Miller, the American Indian ship's cook, and "Chips," the black ship's carpenter from Grand Cayman Island. Both of them, assigned to the midship machine guns, have pulled themselves up the ladders and vaulted into the gun tubs.

CHAPTER 9

AIR ACTION

SOME NINE HOURS LATER, GRAND ADMIRAL RAEDER meets with his staff in Berlin to consider the situation. Circumstances favor an attack by the *Tirpitz*. As of last report Tovey's heavy ships, including the aircraft carrier *Victorious*, are almost 300 miles from the convoy. So far, so good, from the German point of view.

Raeder gives his okay for the last phase of Operation Knight's Move to begin. The *Tirpitz* and the *Hipper*, standing by at Trondheim, are authorized to sail at 8 P.M. They are to proceed to Vestifjord, then Altenfjord, a deep water port below Hammerfest, where they will await the attack order. Hitler must personally approve this order.

But even as Raeder and his staff deliberate at this morning parley, reconnaissance planes are taking off from Norway to continue the hourly tracking of PQ 17. Soon they can be heard aboard ship, buzzing in the fog nearby. One of them is a Blohm & Voss 138 seaplane. Nicknamed "the Flying Shoe," the three-engine recco craft is slow, but perfect for loping along the edges of convoys. The "Shoes" have guns and sometimes carry six small bombs, but their main work is snooping.

Noon comes and goes. Tension builds steadily in the ships due to the continual buzzing in the fog and the occasional glimpses of the clumsy seaplanes. Then, at 3:10 P.M., Broome's escort vessels signal frantically: "Submarine attack!" The first strike is from beneath, not above, the glassy water as six U-boats from Narvik try to break through the diamond defense. Two torpedoes lay a chain of bubbles from beyond the escort screen, and the captain of the *SS Bellingham* turns the ship 45 degrees to avoid them. They skid by harmlessly, passing other ships as well.

From the *River Afton,* Commodore Dowding orders the entire convoy to assume a zig-zag course. Turning one way, then the next, the ships will be more difficult to hit. Radio operators on the ships hear the U-boats begin to send out a signal of steady pitch. Broome knows instantly what it means: the subs are now acting as homing stations, enabling the aircraft to zero in on the convoy's position through the spotty weather.

The signals continue, and at about 6:30 P.M. the attack comes. Four Heinkel 115's—each carrying aerial torpedoes—roar in, two from the port quarter, a pair from the starboard side. Twin-engine float planes with a capacity of a ton of bombs or torpedoes, the Heinkels' usual attack speed is just under 200 miles an hour. They come in on PQ 17 chattering machine gun bullets and dropping explosives.

The entire convoy lights up with pom-pom and Oerlikon fire. Lighter guns burp away. The gunners are trigger happy in this first sea-air action, and there is as much danger to the convoy from the ships' batteries as there is from the air. Shells whistle across masts.

Ensign Carraway unleashes a .37-mm tank gun, firing to port. It works beautifully. His .30-mm machine guns are also popping at the enemy. But a quick glance tells him that the bullets are bouncing off the Heinkels, not penetrating them.

One Heinkel levels at the *Azerbaijan*, its .20-mm cannon spraying across the Russian tanker and into the nearby rescue ship *Zamalek*. Her sister ship *Zaafaran*, firing point-blank, makes a hit, and the German plane staggers down the length of the column to plunge into the sea, amidst cheers from the other ships.

The *Offa* signals: "Torpedo coming toward convoy." An outlying Heinkel has dropped it. The slender missile glides harmlessly through a gap between the ships, while its delivery aircraft turns on speed to climb away from the heavy ack-ack fire. The noise is deafening.

Meanwhile the downed Heinkel, its tail sticking out of the water, detaches a rubber raft. The men in the ships in the outboard port column, near the lead, watch, fascinated, as the daring pilot of another German float plane lands by the wreckage. Gunbursts hit the water around the plane as the destroyers open fire. Three survivors are pulled aboard nonetheless and the rescuing Heinkel takes off again, dodging shellfire. There are mixed emotions in PQ 17 about the deed.

Finally the "All clear" signal is issued and the ships plod on. It is miraculous that not one has been lost to enemy action thus far. Three men on the *Zamalek* have been injured by shrapnel. Otherwise PQ 17 is completely unscratched.

But as dinner plates clink, belatedly, in the crew's mess-rooms and officers' saloons on all the ships, a Blohm & Voss snooper plane takes up station several miles from the starboard column of the convoy.

Later that night, Carraway writes in his diary:

My crew has been great. They were up for nearly 24 hours without sleep and stayed on duty until the attacks stopped at about 8:30 tonight. I dropped off in the wardroom [the dining saloon] and snoozed for about two hours. The crew fell like flies and are sleeping everywhere and anywhere. On the deck, at their guns, in bunks and chairs. One is snoring on the messroom table, his head on his .45.

The convoy maneuvers on throughout the night.

On the Norwegian coast, quite another maneuver has begun. The *Tirpitz,* along with the heavy cruiser *Hipper* and some destroyers, has sailed from Trondheim on schedule and is paralleling PQ 17's northerly course. The ships are gingerly picking their way up the Leads, a tricky passage between the coast and the offshore islands.

CHAPTER 10

TURN BACK?

THE COURSE OF PQ 17 IS ALTERED AT 7 A.M. THIS morning of July 3. The ships will take a route more directly north, hugging the west-lying ice fields and passing between Bear Island and Spitsbergen into the Barents Sea. It is better, Broome and Dowding agree, to cope with icebergs than with Nazi aircraft from Norway. The convoy will stay as far out of bomber range as possible.

Ice reconnaissance the previous day has indicated that the channel is now about 90 miles wide, giving the convoy plenty of room to make the passage. Bear Island is scheduled to be abeam close to midnight.

In midmorning Admiral Hamilton, still hiding in the murk with his cruisers about 50 miles from the convoy, decides it is time to let the Germans know of his presence. The cruisers may be a deterrent from sending the *Tirpitz* to sea. Hamilton wheels around and closes in on the convoy to begin patrolling only 25 miles away, hoping to expose his ships to any U-boats or recco planes in the area. Before very long his wish is granted; the Germans spot him. A wireless message clicks toward Norway.

Admiral Raeder and his commanders are now aware of all the Allied units at sea in northern waters. However, another sighting of Hamilton's ships seems to indicate the presence of an aircraft carrier among the cruisers. This false information is also passed on. The German naval staff is inclined to discount the report of a carrier so close to the convoy, yet they cannot rule the possibility out.

In the convoy itself the morning passes quietly enough, almost pleasantly, in the thick mist. Gunners and lookouts relax in the steel tubs and on the bridge wings, in the crow's nests and on the bows. A routine day seems to be shaping up.

It is not routine for the intelligence experts, though. In the early afternoon a British Spitfire drops down through the clouds over Asafjord to take a quick look and several photographs. Earlier fears are confirmed: the *Tirpitz* and the *Hipper* have indeed departed, along with their destroyers. The information is passed on quickly to the Citadel at Whitehall.

Now the game of wits begins in earnest in London, Berlin,

and Norway. For the Allies the question is, *What are the intentions of the enemy?* Commander Denning has his work cut out for him. For the Germans: *Now that the Allies know the Tirpitz is under way, what countermeasures will they take?*

In Berlin on this warm summer afternoon, Grand Admiral Raeder and his staff are once again meeting to decide whether to send the *Tirpitz* into action. The battleship is now at Vestifjord, awaiting orders to proceed to Altenfjord. According to the latest information Raeder has, Admiral Tovey's force is some 300 miles southwest of the convoy. It offers no immediate threat. Hamilton's ships, so near the convoy, *are* a threat, though, especially if the admiral has a carrier from which he can launch aircraft.

As the clock ticks on and no decision is made, Admiral Schneiwind, aboard the *Tirpitz*, fumes and paces. He wants to sail the battleship to Altenfjord now. But Raeder is hesitant to make even this safe a move without approval from Hitler.

As more communications fly back and forth between Berlin, Narvik, and the Naval Group North command at Kiel, Schneiwind resolves to take matters into his own hands. Defiantly he steams the warships toward Altenfjord. There he can wait for further orders and put to sea within hours.

While the Germans hang between desire for action and the firm orders of Hitler to proceed with utmost caution, PQ 17 moves slowly onward, steering a zig-zag course between Spitsbergen and Bear Island, staying well to the north on orders from the Admiralty. Jack Broome would dearly love to start making progress east, toward Russia, but Hamilton will not permit it as yet.

At about 9 P.M., Tovey and Hamilton receive a startling message from Whitehall: "*Tirpitz, Hipper* and three destroyers have left Trondheim." Commander Broome and Commodore Dowding receive the same message, as do the commanders of some of the other escort ships.

In the ack-ack ship *Pozarica,* steaming along several lengths ahead of the *Troubador,* Commander Clive Martin remarks, "It might be better for the convoy to turn back to Iceland while there is still time." Martin has no desire to tangle with 15-inch guns.

Admiral Hamilton reacts in another way. He turns his cruisers toward the convoy, determined to show again his presence to German recco pilots. In less than two hours his wish is once more granted. A Blohm & Voss spots him and reports by radio that a "battleship, one heavy and two light cruisers, plus destroyers" are in close support of PQ 17. It is another error of vision—there is no battleship in Hamilton's force.

Once again the German strategists are thrown into confusion. If an Allied battleship is indeed in close proximity to the convoy, they will have to change their plans for Operation Knight's Move. The naval staff, now worried even more about the possible strength of British forces, presses for further information.

At midnight, the young third mate of the SS *Troubador* scrawls in the log:

Steaming in company with other ships of the convoy. Sea, calm. Wind, estimated 5 knots west. Considerable ice conditions. Fog to starboard.

Most of the other inhabitants of the *Troubador* are asleep, but Ensign Carraway is wide awake in his tiny cabin, writing at his desk.

Friday, July 3—Thank God for the beautiful, murky, pasty, thick, pea-soup fog. Thick, lovely, impenetrable fog. After I wrote last night, I turned the last of the crew in and went to the bridge to finish the night out. They slept wherever they fell until breakfast, then ate like pigs, washed up and went out to man their guns.

But the fog was with us. We ran most of the morning in it, and during the seven hours left of the afternoon two German scout planes found us and circled us for an hour or so but left in time for supper. They never attacked at all but circled far out from the convoy, near the water because of the low-hanging clouds.

Part of the day there was a British plane with us, too, a relic launched from one of the cruisers. He wasn't much protection but guided the convoy and looked for subs. He made us feel good, anyway.

We stood shortened, lightened watches today and many of the gunners spent all hours off just sleeping. Every time a German would show up and head for the convoy, we'd give the alarm. They never came close enough for us to think of firing. One is still flying around over us but can't see the water. A heavy fog closed in again about 11 o'clock and is tight as a blanket around us now.

During the quiet of morning, I took a much-needed bath, washed my hair and some clothing, and got into a fresh outfit and went to bed. I slept several hours today, about six I guess, all told, but then I'd been up for 36 hours without more than catnaps. I felt better, needless to say.

The steward gave me half a coconut pie. He also slipped me half an apple pie. Then an apple dumpling.

The cruiser escort that we were supposed to have has never shown up. They are not far away, as evidenced by the float plane, but we haven't seen them. And the battlewagon and aircraft carrier have never shown their noses that I know of. But at that, we're four or five days out of Murmansk, seven out of Archangel, and there hasn't been a scratch as yet.

We are in iceberg waters now, and today and tonight passed several of them, about as big as ships. They are beautifully colored. Blue, green and white. They stand out in the cold, calm water like perfect pears. They are rounded smooth by wind and water.

Sadder was the sighting of objects drifting in the sea. Oars, furniture, timbers. Debris of all kinds. From ships lost in other convoys. Probably the last one. It must have been about here that Gib [a friend] caught it.

Good night.

CHAPTER 11

A NOISY FOURTH

LESS THAN TWO HOURS LATER, COMMANDER BROOME
signals all escort captains from the *Keppel:* "Enemy aircraft
attacking on starboard side." It is just past 2 A.M., July 4.

Radar has picked up an incoming flight. General quarters is
sounded on all ships, tumbling Carraway from his bunk,
sending bleary-eyed gunners to the tubs, arousing beefing
merchant sailors to pass ammunition.

The men can hear the aircraft but cannot see them. Fortunately, the fog is as heavy as when they turned in. The surface
of the sea is like a sheet of undulating gray glass, the temperature three degrees above zero.

A German plane blunders onto the convoy, its crew as
surprised as the men on the ships. Guns flame, but the plane
disappears as quickly as it arrived. The next one comes at

about 5 A.M., gliding in with both its engines cut. The ghostly float plane skims toward the outboard column of the *Daniel Morgan, Carlton,* and *Samuel Chase.*

Suddenly torpedoes drop from it, heading directly toward the *Carlton,* that lucky survivor of PQ 16. Then the Heinkel's engines catch and roar again. Its mission accomplished, the plane lifts over the ships, trailing wisps of fog.

The chief mate of the *Carlton* yells for the ship to come hard to port, and slams the engine room telegraph to full astern. The torpedoes slip past her bow as she whistle-blasts a warning to the ships in the next column.

One torpedo is headed directly for the new Liberty ship *Christopher Newport,* leading column No. 8. Her feeble .30-caliber machine guns open fire on the yellow-headed projectile, but it spears on, hitting in the engine room, opening a massive hole and killing instantly three men on watch. The stricken ship loses power and steering simultaneously.

In the confusion, Ensign Carraway is certain that the torpedoed ship is the SS *Benjamin Harrison,* also a new Liberty. The ships are identical in type and at sea do not carry name boards; it is difficult to distinguish one Liberty from another. Carraway's good friend Ensign Fred Thompson is gunnery officer on the *Harrison.* Watching the stricken ship, Carraway wonders if Thompson, whom he met at gunnery school, has survived.

The rescue vessel *Zamalek*, dropping two of her lifeboats, surges toward the *Christopher Newport*. Three escort ships also converge on her to discourage submarine attack and to determine if she can be saved.

Commander Broome is directing operations from the *Keppel*, which is, as usual, moving ahead. The majority of the escort units, especially the *Keppel*, cannot abandon their first reponsibility to the entire convoy for the sake of one crippled vessel.

In less than a half hour, the *Zamalek* has taken aboard forty-seven survivors of the *Christopher Newport*, the first casualty of PQ 17 by enemy action. The sailors do not even have wet feet—a testimony to the great value of the small rescue ships.

Commodore Dowding, on the bridge of the *River Afton*, has little to say about this first loss. If anything, luck has been with them so far, and he hopes it will hold. The convoy has not changed its basic course by a degree for several hours; it has not slowed a single knot. Dowding is satisfied.

The abandoned and sinking *Newport* will soon be over the horizon, prey for any German sub or aircraft that might want to finish her off.

Another air attack develops at 6 A.M., and still another at 8. Both are thwarted. The weather is still kind; fog is helping the Allies.

Promptly at eight o'clock, the usual time for raising flags on

81

ships, the American *Hoosier,* a forlorn old tramp in the port outboard column, lowers her grimy and tattered flag as enemy aircraft mill around in the mist above. For a moment, to the men on ships nearby who have taken notice, it seems an act of cowardice. Then a new, fresh, sparkling flag breaks out aboard the *Hoosier*.

Almost as if on cue, all the American ships in PQ 17 hoist new Stars and Stripes. The weather is not quite right for picnics, but it is after all Independence Day, 900 miles from the North Pole.

Although the Fourth of July has no significance on German calendars, it looks as if this might be a promising day for the Third Reich. Clear skies are forecast ahead of the convoy: good bomber weather. The ships will no longer be able to hide in the fog.

The British certainly have no reason to celebrate the date their American colonies broke away in 1776. They will spend this Saturday at work, both at sea and at Whitehall. The Citadel is a very busy place.

Commander Denning's unit has received a report from a reliable agent that German warships intend to attack the convoy somewhere between latitudes 15 and 30 degrees east. Already Sir Dudley Pound is preparing for a long staff conference. Subject: PQ 17 and the *Tirpitz*.

But on U.S. ships in the convoy and on Yankee-flagged vessels riding with Admirals Tovey and Hamilton, the holiday is celebrated in small ways, provoking memories of home and family, of firecrackers, watermelon, hot dogs, and hamburgers. Many of the men grew up in the 1920s and 1930s, when small-town America made the most of July 4.

In midmorning, commanders on the Allied ships receive a signal from the Admiralty:

Visual reconnaissance, confirmed by photos, of Trondheim reported that no heavy units were present. Admiralty appreciates that:

(A) A move by enemy heavy units to the north is in progress.

(B) This threatens the convoy, but there is no immediate danger.

(C) Weather is favorable for the convoy to eastward.

(D) Admiralty is therefore taking no action at present but is awaiting developments.

Among the matters of concern in the Citadel is the fact that there has been no late reconnaissance of the Norwegian fjords, primarily because of bad weather. However, the experts believe that the pocket battleships *Scheer* and *Lützow* are already at Altenfjord. Perhaps the *Tirpitz* and the *Hipper* have joined them, perhaps not. A third possibility is that all four enemy ships are at sea and steaming into the Allied convoy lanes.

Admiral Hamilton has been under orders not to take his cruisers too far to the north or east, where they would be exposed to shore-based air and concentrated U-boat attack. Hamilton is now reaching the limits set by the Admiralty yet wants to stay with the convoy. He turns his force toward it just before noon.

When the big British ships loom protectively over the horizon about 1 P.M., the spirits of the men soar. In the words of Captain Stone of the SS *Olopana*, "It was good to see the heavy ships out there. We all felt we had a chance to get through now."

Hamilton makes a decision to stay close to the convoy for at least another day, just in case the German heavies do come out from Norway.

In fact, the German warships now have that easy capability. The *Tirpitz* along with the *Hipper* now swing at anchor at Altenfjord, at the north tip of Norway. They are standing by, ready to sail. Steam is up, and ammunition is on the lifts from the magazines.

At the British Admiralty, the day-long meeting between the First Sea Lord and his staff has been under way for several hours. At one point Admiral Pound asks an officer whether the merchant ships can communicate with Allied commands if it is necessary to scatter them and let them run independently for port.

The answer is affirmative. Each ship has a set of Merchant Signal Codes, or MerSigs. But most of the officers present find his question disquieting. If the ships were to scatter, each would have to defend itself alone against certain U-boat and air attack.

CHAPTER 12

A CRAZY TORPEDO

ALL THIS DAY PREPARATIONS HAVE BEEN UNDER way at the German air base at Bardufoss, located between Narvik and Tromsö, to deal PQ 17 a death blow. General Stumpff and the Luftwaffe, having no great love for the German Navy and much impatience with the admirals for delaying the *Tirpitz* strike, decide to attack before the convoy is out of easy air range.

Twin-engine Heinkel 111's—torpedo bombers—will be used. They are land-based aircraft, and no strangers to the British. London had a taste of them during the Battle of Britain in 1940. With a range of 1,700 miles, they can carry plenty of gas to make the round trip to the convoy, estimated to be less than 500 miles away. Some Junker 88's—high-level bombers—will go along to occupy the attention of the convoy while the low-level Heinkels thrust in to drop torpedoes.

The Bardufoss squadrons roar off, but even before they clear the Norwegian coast, PQ 17 is already under air attack. Heinkel float planes from another northern base are closing in on the ships. Just before 5 P.M., Commander Broome signals his escort ships to wedge in, to mass their firepower.

The escorts dart toward the zig-zagging columns of merchant vessels, each flying "Q" flags to warn the ships of an air strike. Sirens echo across the peace. Luckily, bright sun has, for the moment, given way to overcast.

The float planes begin buzzing about the edges of the convoy, looking for opportunities to whip in and drop torpedoes. When they veer too close, Broome's ships fill the sky with ack-ack. For more than two hours the German aircraft dog the convoy without success, then drone off.

It is only a lull. The constant-pitch tone being sent by snooper seaplanes and subs indicates that a larger force is homing in on the convoy. The aircraft from Bardufoss are about to arrive.

At this moment the thin cloud layer is still above the convoy, but some fifteen miles ahead sunshine surrounds Admiral Hamilton's cruisers as they steam along, duplicating PQ 17's horse-drill, zig-zag course.

For nearly two hours the U.S. destroyer *Wainwright*,

detached from the cruisers temporarily, has been trying to line up with the oiler *Aldersdale* to take fuel on board. The float planes have stymied those plans as the *Wainwright,* with fierce and accurate gunfire, helped to send them home.

After the aircraft departed, Broome blinked a message to the *Wainwright:* "Was the original 4th July as noisy as this?"

Captain Donald Moon, commander of the cruiser support screen—the destroyers escorting the cruisers—blinked back: "I wasn't there but guess negative."

Now, Moon's destroyer is moving down the starboard outside column of ships, past the *Samuel Chase* and *Daniel Morgan,* listening to the ominous steady-pitch dot-dash on the radio direction finder. The *Wainwright* spots the torpedo planes on the horizon astern, to the starboard quarter of the convoy. They look like a flight of low-flying geese. Then other ships see them. The bleat of loudspeakers cuts across the convoy: "Stand by! Stand by!"

The enemy aircraft are still five miles away. Starboard and aft guns swivel and point; gun crews wait. Lookouts begin to count the growing dots in the sky. *Five planes . . . ten . . . fifteen . . . twenty.*

Actually, there are twenty-three torpedo bombers readying for attack, some off the starboard quarter, others flashing ahead to hit at the convoy lead.

Captain Moon orders the *Wainwright* to turn to meet the

second group head on, picking up the speed to 32 knots, then opening fire at very long range on the aircraft moving in toward the rear of the convoy. PQ 17 is now emerging into bright sun and brilliant blue sky.

Suddenly the blue heaven is filled with red flashes and puffs of black smoke. The din is ear-shattering, as any man with a possible target in sight triggers his gun. Approximately 500 guns are firing simultaneously.

As the Heinkels thunder in, barely 60 feet above the tops of the waves—the normal approach for torpedo attack—Captain Moon swerves the *Wainwright* sharply to bring every gun possible to bear broadsides. The ship is now about 4,000 yards out from the convoy, on the direct flight path of the enemy. Then the *Wainwright* almost vanishes in smoke as her gun barrels spout red. The destroyer heels over from the kick of the guns.

In the face of Moon's barrage, all but one aircraft drop their torpedoes short of the destroyer, where they are of little threat to the convoy. The final aircraft flies on, into the hail of hot steel, and as it trips its first torpedo it takes two positive hits from the *Wainwright* guns. A second torpedo flops into the water as the Heinkel, now smoking and beginning to burn, angles into the sea. Moon finds himself "combing," or dodging, the torpedoes.

As the *Wainwright* returns to the convoy, passing within 50 yards of the *Troubador*, Ensign Carraway leads a cheering

90

section at the ship's rail. The men "waved and hooted like students at a high school football game."

Carraway's diary later says:

We stood by the guns a few minutes longer and I decided the worst was over. The men had lost much sleep lately so I started around and secured the men, with instructions to rest in full gear, ready to return to battle stations at a second's notice. . . .

I smile when I remember how Sparks Sauls, the fellow from the woods of South Carolina, went around with me grinning because he had seen some good fireworks on the 4th of July. He had been worried that the day would pass in the dull, dreary convoy atmosphere. He bragged to everyone he saw, especially to the foreigners, about the way the U.S. tincan had sent Jerry [the Germans] hightailing home, and how Jerry had missed on every shot so far except one, and that was a lucky shot in the fog that just happened to hit. If this was war, then he liked it. Jerry was not a problem at sea, he said. We could take care of a dozen [attacks] like that. . . .

Seconds later, Sparks Sauls' chatter is stopped by a shout from Chips, the black carpenter. He has spotted a plane coming in from the south.

Carraway yells, "Man your guns," and scampers to the bridge while Sauls runs for cover. On the bridge wing, Carraway trains his binoculars to the rear of the convoy and sees not one plane but twelve. They appear to be maneuvering into attack position, directly into the rear of the convoy.

Speaking into the gunnery communications system, the ensign reads off the number of planes approaching and the direction they are coming from, then issues instructions to the tank gunners. He tells the Lewis machine gunners to hold fire until the planes are overhead.

One plane has taken the lead and is heading straight for the middle of the convoy. The pilot is flying several hundred yards ahead of the others, barely above mast height at an altitude of about 200 feet. Carraway cannot help but admire the pilot's bravery. Then more than a hundred guns open up at the Heinkel simultaneously.

Carraway watches as the heavy red tracers from a tank gun begin to curve out, missing the aircraft by feet. The loud, hollow "bung-bung-bung" of the tank gun is different from the sounds of the other guns in the convoy. One shot sails through the mast of a British ship in the column and then tears into the Heinkel's after fuselage.

In the middle of the convoy, the plane releases its load. Three long, slender, cigar-shaped torpedoes drop from the belly of the aircraft and dive into the water. Carraway, in the starboard bridge gun tub, is transfixed by them for a moment, his attention diverted from the aircraft.

Then a shout goes up, and he glances at the plane again. A red glow is widening in the forward part of the fuselage; black smoke trails behind it. The Heinkel careens into the water ahead of the convoy while the lead ships pour bullets into the flaming wreckage.

The other planes break formation, banking left and right. Carraway orders the after gun trained on them. Then he looks toward the flying bridge. He later notes in his diary:

There was Salvesen, calm as an oak in all the confusion. The deck was a madhouse. All the crew, except the few faithful down in the engine room, were running around, yelling and screaming in 40 tongues, looking like wild men in their arctic clothing, clumsy life-jackets, silly shrapnel helmets, gas masks and addled brains. I was proud of the captain.

Three planes are now close to the *Troubador,* and Carraway opens fire with his machine gun.

I chose one and let go with my puny .30-caliber. His belly was to us, and all four of our .30-calibers were pouring it hard into him. I could see the bullets hit. Some vanished from sight. Others bounced off the steel armor plating.

The plane comes directly across the stern of the *Troubador*, close enough for the men in the after gun tub to feel the heat from its exhaust. Carraway loses sight of the aircraft for a moment as it is blocked from vision by the deckhouse.

I turned to look for another target. A loud, roaring explosion shook me and I paid attention to it. It was one of the big Liberty ships, the William Hooper. *Two or three torpedoes had hit her near the stern. The whole after end was blown off.*

The *Hooper* is directly opposite the *Troubador*, 600 yards away. They've been neighbors for a week.

Two other planes come within range of the *Troubador*'s .30-calibers while the tank guns bung away at more distant targets. The two nearby aircraft drop their torpedoes.

Carraway's diary notes:

Then my knees buckled. Headed for our side was a torpedo. What chilled me was the apparent point of contact, directly below the midships house on the starboard side. I screamed, "Torpedo on the starboard beam!" . . .

Carraway hops from his gun tub, yelling, "Hard aport!" to Salvesen in an effort to have the ship turned away from the missile.

Then I ran aft to the tank and yelled into it, to Brannen and Busbin, "Get out, torpedo!" They couldn't hear me. I started to climb up on the tank, but then saw the torpedo coming into the side of the ship. I dropped to my knees and grabbed a nearby hatch cover and held on, kneeling as if in prayer, waiting for the explosion. It didn't come. The tinfish either missed the ship forward or went under it. After a few seconds, I ran back to the gun tub. Crew members were yelling and screaming. A few had fallen on their faces, blabbering crazily. . . .

The acoustical torpedo, homing on noise from the ship's engines, is now on the port side, gliding on the surface in an arc near the stern. It is of the type that is set to travel in a 100-yard circle, exploding on impact with any hard surface. Two crewmen at the stern, a Portuguese and a Spaniard, are gesturing at it and shouting. Later, Carraway will learn that they are yelling, "Go away! Go away!"

There is little comedy elsewhere. Bill Lawson, the big, blond kid from Virginia, an alternate radio operator, is firing burst after burst of .30-caliber bullets from his portside gun tub, attempting to deflect the tinfish from the ship.

On the flying bridge, Captain Salvesen is giving orders to the helmsman, trying to guide the ship away from the torpedo. Carraway later records: "Both were calm, cool and collected, logical—the only two on the ship that were."

Climbing back into his gun tub, Carraway sights on the torpedo as it circles around to hit the starboard side. He aims head on, hoping to explode it in the water. Before he can mash the trigger, the slender missile suddenly stops, turns up on end, and sinks tail first beneath the surface.

It was a very crazy torpedo.

Other missiles slither through the lanes between the ships, missing one vessel and then another—though not for long. First the *Navarino,* in the fourth column, is hit. She staggers and tilts to starboard as water gushes into a black, gaping hole in her hull. Some of her crew begin leaping overboard, not waiting to board the lifeboat that is being lowered from her port side.

Almost simultaneously, flame rolls back across the Russian *Azerbaijan*, covering her female gunners from view. A torpedo has holed her. Heavy black smoke almost blots her out of sight.

Ships behind the *Navarino* and *Azerbaijan* steer carefully past them, their crews gazing at the swimming men and at the dangling lifeboats and the rafts plummeting down. The rescue ships now move out at flank speed toward the stricken vessels, dropping pick-up boats en route.

As the pall of smoke finally clears over the *Azerbaijan,* the men spot her female gun crew in the bow tub. They are still loading and firing, though there are few targets now.

The wreckage of the Heinkel that led the daring strike is still afloat, its tail poking up above the water. Men aboard the ships in the outside column curse the bomber crew as they clamber into a rubber raft. A destroyer picks them up. The next stop for them is an Allied prisoner of war camp.

The attack is over. It has lasted only a few minutes. Three ships have been hit; two are sinking. Two enemy aircraft have been downed.

The convoy steams steadily on, and soon the *Azerbaijan* signals she'll join up. Still trailing smoke, she limps toward the convoy while the crew begin preparations to put an emergency patch over the torpedo hole. Before long, she is back on station as if nothing had happened.

As food is dished out on all the ships, spirits are high. The convoy has survived a massive air attack, and two German planes have been downed. The Luftwaffe is not invincible after all!

Commander Broome later remarks, "Steaming back through the convoy was a tonic. Ships were still on station, looking prouder than ever."

Carraway's diary note concerns the *Troubador*, naturally.

We got by the torpedo with a combination of good marksmanship, smart maneuvering and good luck. I think Lawson saved the day.

CHAPTER 13

QUESTIONS IN THE CITADEL

AT ABOUT THE TIME THE HEINKELS BREAK OFF attack and head back for Bardufoss, the First Sea Lord is moving down into the depths of the Citadel. With him are key staff members. The day-long conference has not brought about a decision on how to cope with the *Tirpitz*.

It is possible that Prime Minister Winston Churchill has been told of the battleship's movement north, though there is no record of it. There is a strong bond between Sir Dudley Pound and the Prime Minister. Churchill trusts this very experienced and capable officer.

Admiral Pound talks with Paymaster-Commander Denning about the situation, which has changed little since morning. Bad weather has prevented aerial reconnaissance. Neither has Denning received word from agents that the *Tirpitz* is at

Altenfjord, though he believes it to be a likely spot for her to refuel before sailing into the convoy lanes.

The brief conversation in the dimly lit room was not recorded, but according to various people's memories of it, Pound asks Denning, "Do you know if the *Tirpitz* has put to sea?"

Denning replies that if she is at sea they will know very shortly, within four to six hours. (There is an agent in a village near Altenfjord.)

"Can you assure me that the *Tirpitz* is at anchorage in Altenfjord?"

Denning replies that he cannot.

Pound then asks Denning if the *Tirpitz* is ready to go to sea, assuming she is at Altenfjord.

The Paymaster-Commander says that he believes she will not leave within the next few hours. He reasons that if she were weighing anchor, her escorting destroyers would have already put to sea, searching for Allied submarines along her intended route. British and Russian subs patrolling off North Cape have seen no German destroyers.

Admiral Pound and his staff then go to the submarine tracking room. There Pound is told that the U-boat situation is critical. PQ 17 is certain to come under heavy attack by enemy subs; Hamilton's cruisers are in danger, too.

As the high-ranking officers return to daylight and the First

Sea Lord's office, they know these things: (1) Denning is not absolutely certain that the *Tirpitz* hasn't sailed. (2) The submarine expert has warned of a critical situation developing.

Admiral Pound asks each member of his staff what he thinks should be done. With the exception of the Vice Chief of Naval Staff, Vice Admiral Sir Henry Moore, all the officers are against scattering the convoy.

But apparently the First Sea Lord had already made up his mind. He closes his eyes for a few seconds in deep thought and then issues his orders. The decision is a momentous one, and he makes it without consulting either Admiral Tovey or Admiral Hamilton, his at-sea commanders: "Secret. Most immediate. Cruiser force withdraw to westward at high speed. . . ."

To all three commanders at sea—Tovey, Hamilton, and Broome—the message has one clear meaning: the Admiralty has solid information that the *Tirpitz* will soon invade the Barents Sea. Why else would the cruisers have to withdraw at flank speed? A second message, arriving a few minutes later, confirms their feelings: "Secret. Immediate. Owing to threat from surface ships convoy is to disperse and proceed to Russian ports."

"Convoy is to disperse" means that the ships are to break formation but head in a group for Murmansk and Archangel. Vice Admiral Moore points this out to the First Sea Lord, and the wording is immediately changed. A third message is sent: "Secret. Most immediate. My 21.23B of the 4th. Convoy is to scatter."

"Scatter," of course, means to fan out. The ships are to stay as far away from each other as possible. Clustered together, they offer easy targets for the guns of the *Tirpitz,* and no weapon in the convoy can match the range and size of the battleship's guns. From 20 miles away, with the help of spotting aircraft, the *Tirpitz* can sink any ship of choice.

Although it is not completely clear to his associates, Admiral Pound has apparently based his decision on this factor plus a fear of losing Hamilton's cruisers to subs, or even to the *Tirpitz*. England cannot afford to lose *any* heavy warships at this time.

Nonetheless, in this situation, "scatter" is a terrifying order.

In the Citadel, Paymaster-Commander Denning and his associates are shocked. For the first time Admiral Pound has not accepted their intelligence estimates. As of this hour, they have no firm evidence that the *Tirpitz* has put to sea. The "scatter" signal, as they well know, means that the ships of PQ 17 will be at the mercy of Nazi U-boats and aircraft.

The shock naturally is even greater on the bridges of the Allied ships at sea. Of the last message, Commander Broome later says, "This one was lethal. It exploded in my hand."

In the Citadel, Denning urges his immediate superior to

plead with the First Sea Lord to reconsider his decision. He does, but is told that the order must stand. Admiral Pound is apparently convinced that the *Tirpitz* has left Altenfjord and is steaming steadily toward PQ 17. Besides, Winston Churchill has already been notified of Pound's decision.

Commander Broome, too, is convinced that the enemy's masts will appear on the horizon at any moment. He decides to attach his destroyers to Admiral Hamilton's force to assist the cruisers in a gunnery duel with the *Tirpitz* group.

On the *River Afton,* Commodore Dowding at first refuses to believe that the convoy is to be consigned to the Nazi chopping block. He cannot bring himself to tell the other ships that, after such a valiant fight two hours previously, they are to be abandoned.

He pauses a few minutes and then communicates by voice with Commander Broome. After that, he reluctantly hoists the signal to scatter, knowing that all the merchant skippers in the convoy will be stunned.

Broome then orders the destroyers *Fury, Offa, Wilton,* and *Leamington* to join his *Keppel* and Hamilton's cruisers. The other smaller escort ships will have to proceed independently to Archangel. The skippers of the British subs decide to remain in the area for the time being to await the *Tirpitz.* They will attempt to torpedo the dreadnought.

As the *River Afton* begins to surge ahead of the rest of the ships, taking the lead in the scatter procedure, a saddened Dowding signals to Broome: "Many thanks. Good luck and good hunting." By now, Dowding is also convinced that the destroyers and cruisers will soon be engaged in battle with the *Tirpitz*.

Broome sends a message to Dowding, and to the smaller escort ships—the corvettes, minesweepers, trawlers, ack-ack ships, and rescue vessels: "Sorry to leave you like this. Good luck. Looks like a bloody business."

As the *Keppel* turns back through the convoy, now beginning slowly to break up, Broome is occupied with disturbing thoughts. He later recalls: "My impression was that the fog bank to the westward, where the cruisers were approaching, was probably where the enemy was hiding."

Because of a lack of time and of precise knowledge of what is happening, Commodore Dowding has given his merchant ships no explanation for the sudden change in plans. None of the civilian captains is aware of the threat of the *Tirpitz,* and they are puzzled and worried. Captain Salvesen curses roundly, and later says, "None of us would believe it." In his diary, Carraway writes:

We have been brought into the middle of the fire and then told that there is no water.

Salvesen swings the *Troubador* out of line, taking a north-westerly course toward Spitsbergen, a group of bleak and practically uninhabited Norwegian islands lying between Norway's North Cape and Greenland, on the very edge of the Arctic Ocean. Beyond Spitsbergen is the North Pole. Salvesen, his chief mate, Ericksen, and his chief engineer, Ingebretsen, have sailed these waters since they were boys. They know of hiding places along the coast of Spitsbergen, and all agree that the best chance to stay alive is to come to anchor, wait until the main German attacks are over, and then sneak off to Russia's White Sea and the port of Archangel. Soon the *Troubador* is steaming alone in light fog.

On the other merchant ships there is great uncertainty and hot anger. Able-bodied Seaman Serge Kolence stands on the bow of the SS *Honomu* yelling at the destroyer *Offa* as she begins to pull away. "Come back!" he shouts.

The merchantman *Bellingham* is close behind the rescue ship *Rathlin*. Enraged, Captain Mortensen rings the engine room, ordering his chief engineer to "give us every bit of steam you can squeeze out of those boilers." Then he orders the helmsman to steer on the *Rathlin*'s stern. Soon the *Bellingham* has built up to 14 quivering knots, clinging to the British escort ship.

From the *Rathlin* comes a signal: "Please get away." She

wants no part of being near a loaded cargo vessel the Germans are certain to attack.

Mortensen doesn't even bother to answer the signal. He just stares grimly at the foam beneath the *Rathlin*'s stern.

The scattering merchant ships are almost 300 miles from the nearest Russian port, the besieged city of Murmansk. They are almost directly off the tip of North Cape. Fields of heavy ice, presenting a natural barrier, and the Spitsbergen Islands are north and west, over their left shoulder. South and east is the certainty of German U-boats and aircraft.

Yet the closest Allied land is to the southeast, through the danger zone: the large, pickle-shaped, barren Russian islands of Novaya Zemlya, split by a narrow but navigable channel named Matochkin Shar. The channel empties into the Kara Sea but is known to be ice-blocked most of the year at the eastern opening, toward the Russian mainland. Some of the most forbidding lands on earth border the Kara Sea.

Despite the prospect of enemy action en route, some skippers decide to run for Novaya Zemlya, though they do not have charts for these waters. They plan to hide in Matochkin Shar. Others set a more direct course, toward the mouth of the White Sea. No route looks safe. By midnight, the sea approximately 230 miles off Norway's North Cape is chaotic. Singly or in pairs, the ships edge along their chosen routes to safety.

Almost at the same hour the *Troubador,* still heading for Spitsbergen, runs into another light fog. Just before it closes down, Carraway spots two merchant ships nearby. One is the SS *Pankraft,* with his friend Harry Vawter aboard. Carraway wishes that the *Pankraft* would fall in behind the *Troubador.* Vawter would be a good man to have along if bombers attacked.

Also nearby is the big freighter SS *Washington.* Chugging along behind that vessel is a British armed trawler. It is the *Ayrshire,* though Carraway does not know her name at the moment. Then the fog obscures the three ships. In his diary Carraway writes:

We steamed on, nervous still, but resting in the protective blanket.

Three hours later, Admiral Hamilton's heart sinks as he reads a message from the Admiralty. The *Tirpitz* is now believed to be still at Altenfjord. Therefore it is possible that she presents no immediate threat.

This same message hits Commander Broome, on the bridge of the *Keppel,* like a cold fist. He alone made the decision to pull his destroyers away from the convoy and provide added protection to Hamilton's cruisers. Admiral Hamilton agreed, compounding the mistake that had begun in Whitehall.

With deepening despair, Broome signals Hamilton of his readiness to return to the fleeing ships. It is too late—far too late. The *Keppel* has been withdrawing at high speed for almost five hours. Broome could never return in time to herd the merchantmen back into formation. Fuel is another problem. Unless he located the fugitive *Aldersdale* and took on oil, his engines might stop.

The battle is over for Commander Broome and for Admiral Hamilton.

By early morning on July 5, the German high command is baffled. A submarine has spotted the Allied cruisers abruptly turning southwest, moving fast. Just before midnight, a German aircraft reported that the convoy was spreading. Then another aircraft confirmed that PQ 17 appeared to have broken up.

Although he does not know the reasons for the surprising turn of events, Admiral Schmundt decides to take complete advantage of the situation. He orders the Ice Devil subs to attack every Allied merchantman they can find, telling them to keep their eyes open for a return of Hamilton's cruisers.

In Moscow, the Russians have been monitoring the scatter messages, and the British naval representative has been summoned to Soviet naval headquarters for an explanation.

Premier Josef Stalin has been notified that the convoy has been abandoned. He, above all, wants to know why.

From high above in a Nazi recco plane this morning, the scene of the Barents Sea in the pale Arctic light is one of floating steel mice scurrying for safety, laying long, foamy wakes behind them on the still waters.

CHAPTER 14

THE FRIENDLY *AYRSHIRE*

AT ABOUT 12:30 A.M. ON JULY 5, THE FOG LIFTS, and Ensign Carraway searches the waters for signs of the *Pankraft* and *Washington*. They have vanished. Only the smoky little *Ayrshire* is in sight.

Soon the *Ayrshire* steams alongside the *Troubador*, and a man about six feet tall with a ruddy complexion, clad in a heavy brown coat (known as a "convoy coat"), lifts a megaphone to his lips. He speaks in a refined British accent. His voice is very calm and relaxed. He is Lieutenant Leo Gradwell, Royal Navy Reserve, commanding officer of the trawler. In civilian life Gradwell is a lawyer.

He asks Captain Salvesen if he would like some company. The *Ayrshire* carries depth charges and anti-aircraft guns and has a submarine listening device. Though the battered trawler is a tiny vessel, Salvesen and everyone else aboard the *Troubador* welcome at this point any friendly company.

Gradwell instructs the *Troubador* to proceed into the nearby ice fields, where they will make further plans. The presence of the *Ayrshire* and the cool voice of Gradwell lift the spirits of the men of the *Troubador*.

At 1 A.M., they sight another ship, which seems to be wandering around the edge of the ice floes. For a moment Carraway thinks it is the *Pankraft*, and he is on the verge of sending a message to Harry Vawter. In a moment more he is disappointed to learn that it is the SS *Ironclad*, the Hog Islander they saw earlier.

The *Ironclad*, plagued with trouble all the way, has been trying to reach Russia since a February convoy, when she was lost in the fog and returned to Iceland. She's missed two other convoys, one because of engine trouble and another because of mutiny. Gradwell invites the *Ironclad* to join the group. She gladly accepts.

About an hour later Carraway sights another ship. She too appears to be headed for the ice. Through binoculars she looks exactly like the *Pankraft*, and Carraway is again overjoyed at the idea of having Harry Vawter in Lieutenant Gradwell's "private convoy." But when the ship steams closer, Carraway discovers that it is the SS *Silver Sword*.

What a collection of ships, he thinks. They're all old and

feeble. The *Silver Sword* has experienced a mutiny too, in Hvalfjördur. They aren't the most united, happiest group of vessels afloat. But, more important, they *are* afloat.

At about 3:30 A.M., with the stout *Ayrshire* in the lead, all four ships head directly into the drifting ice floes and begin to make their way through them. Gradwell's idea is to take the vessels a short way into the ice to avoid attacks from subs. The U-boats cannot safely surface in the ice, nor can they fire torpedoes at ships in the floes.

Gradwell is not entirely unselfish in his efforts. His main purpose is to attempt to save the vessels. However, on first meeting the *Troubador,* he noticed she was a coal burner, like his own *Ayrshire.* He discreetly inquired if she had plenty of fuel. Gradwell needs some of the *Troubador*'s coal to keep his own engines running.

As this "splinter" convoy seeks safety in the ice, Ensign Carraway drops into his bunk fully clothed and is asleep within minutes.

Another nightless night has passed above the Arctic Circle, and it is 8 A.M. of July 5. The remnants of convoy PQ 17 are moving on various courses.

The British freighter SS *Empire Byron* is steaming alone in the Barents Sea, which is littered to the south and west with debris and oil slicks from the previous day's attacks. Nearby, though not in sight of the *Byron,* is the American ship SS *Peter Kerr.* Far ahead is the SS *Carlton,* the so-called "Jonah" ship.

The *Byron*'s captain, John Wharton, is exhausted, collapsed in his chair in the master's sea cabin just off the bridge. Like all the other masters, he has not slept for almost two days.

Suddenly a single torpedo explodes in the ship's engine room, and within minutes the *Empire Byron* slides beneath the water. Eighteen men die. She is the first of many PQ 17 ships that will be slaughtered this day. The luckless *Carlton* is next, at 9:45 A.M. Three men die, and a number of others are badly injured.

As the *Carlton* settles to the bottom, anchors are coming up at Altenfjord. The *Tirpitz* has finally received orders to prepare for immediate sailing. The heavy British battle units are known to be far away from North Cape. It appears to the German high command that nothing of great danger lies in the path of the world's largest battleship.

There is also activity aboard the cruiser *Hipper,* the pocket battleship *Scheer,* and the seven destroyers and two torpedo boats. This is the German armada that will sail into the Barents Sea to mop up what is left of PQ 17.

At about noon, Admiral Carls issues the order from Kiel for the attack to begin. Operation Knight's Move is a reality. But the *Tirpitz* is already under way, moving toward the open sea. Admiral Schneiwind did not wait for final approval to sail. By 3 P.M. the deadly German battle fleet has emerged from the Leads and sets a northeasterly course in the direction of Novaya Zemlya.

In early afternoon, in the radio shack aboard the *Troubador,* an exhausted Sparks Sauls listens to the frantic messages from other merchant ships, some of which have been under attack for several hours. Carraway stands beside him as the Morse code flows from the receiver and Sparks verbally translates the bad news.

"Heard anything from the *Pankraft*?" Carraway asks.

The radio operator shakes his head.

The freighter *Washington* reports that she's abandoning ship. Eight dive bombers are attacking her, the British *Bolton Castle,* and the Dutch *Paulus Potter* at a point some 50 miles from the *Troubador*'s position.

The *Washington*, loaded with high explosives, goes first. The *Bolton Castle*, also loaded with TNT, then takes one bomb on her foredeck, and the Barents Sea heaves with a red-blue blast. The *Paulus Potter*'s steering gear is knocked out by a bomb and she drifts aimlessly.

Carraway holds his breath as the *Pankraft* begins to

transmit a message that she is under attack. The old ship has been moving north through drifting, broken ice, her firebox sending up black ropes of smoke. In the bright sunshine she is easy to see from the cockpits of the high-level Nazi bombers.

A few minutes later the *Pankraft* reports that she's been hit and is being abandoned. Her position is less than 20 miles from the *Troubador*. Carraway steps out to the bridge to scan the horizon. He sees smoke and hopes that Harry Vawter is okay.

He does not reenter the radio shack. It is heartbreaking to listen to the distress signals.

Sometime later, Gradwell stops the small convoy for a moment. He instructs the *Troubador, Ironclad,* and *Silver Sword* to follow him even deeper into the ice to avoid air attack. Thus far they have been in field ice—broken floes—but now they will enter the solid ice pack itself.

"We were scared stiff," Carraway writes in his diary.

Planes were within twenty miles of us—easy sighting distance, five minutes away by air—and this trawler and our few guns were all that we had. The sky was bright and clear. We could expect twenty-four hours of perfect visibility. We manned the guns and waited. It was awful. Poor Sparks got sick from fear and excitement and threw up over the rail.

An hour passes and the distress signals become less frequent, as the four ships move deeper into the pack ice, finally locating a lead—a long channel of open water. At 6:30 P.M., Lieutenant Gradwell signals the ships to put every drop of white paint available on the starboard sides and decks. It is a brilliant idea. The white paint will camouflage the ships, blending them with the ice and making them almost invisible from the air. With the unpainted sides of the vessels hugging the ice and the white sides facing the open water, they will be able to sneak along the edge of the ice to the east, then turn south to the safety of Novaya Zemlya.

Within minutes, almost every man on board the ships is slopping white paint on midship houses, rails, lifeboats, masts—everywhere. For once there is no shortage of volunteers. It is probably the first time in history that ships have been painted at sea to prevent enemy attack. Ensign Carraway selects a large brush and starts to work.

Later, the *Ayrshire* comes alongside and Gradwell, in a rumpled uniform, leaps aboard the *Troubador* for a "war conference." He is smiling and confident, even cocky. He passes off their predicament by quoting a British war hero who once said, "Not 'My God, there's the enemy,' but 'Thank God, there's the enemy.' " Then, briskly, he asks Captain Salvesen what he'd like to do—head south for Russia, or what?

Salvesen thinks they should move deeper into the ice, finish painting the ships, let the excitement die down for a day or two, then make a run for it.

Gradwell agrees to this plan and suggests that, to save time, bed linen be spread over the decks. Stewards on all the ships begin raiding their supplies. Even tablecloths are donated to Operation Camouflage.

The cause of all the trouble, the *Tirpitz,* has now been at sea since early afternoon, and at 7 P.M. she is sighted by British reconnaissance aircraft. At 8:30, a watch officer aboard the British submarine *Trident* spots her again, through the ship's periscope, and Whitehall is advised.

An hour later, much to the fury of Admiral Schneiwind, the German naval staff sends a message to recall her. She turns and heads back for Norway. With the merchantmen scattered and with German subs and aircraft taking turns at sinking individual ships, there is little need to risk her further.

In an ironic way, she has done her job. Without even firing a shot, she has forced the Allied convoy to scatter. She has made it possible for the subs and aircraft to attack without fear of escort guns. Operation Knight's Move is over.

There is one last vessel to suffer in this long day—the *River Afton,* the comfortable, proud ship that bears the flag of Commodore Dowding. A few minutes past ten, a torpedo slams into her engine room, interrupting her dash to Novaya

Zemlya. Then, as another torpedo hits, the engine room begins to flood. Dowding remains on the ship, ordering his men to hold fast until she actually sinks. A third torpedo crashes into her hull, and Dowding is thrown into the water as the vessel breaks up around him with a heavy loss of life.

With the ship's lifeboats smashed, there are only rafts and a small utility boat to take the survivors 200 miles to shore. Exhausted and dripping wet, Commodore Dowding sits in one of the rafts, contemplating the disaster.

The slaughter of July 5 is over. Eight Allied merchantmen have been lost. More than sixty men are dead. Others, in drifting lifeboats or rafts, are dying. Possibly one German aircraft has been downed; it is a small price for the Luftwaffe to pay.

At about 3 A.M. on July 6, Ensign Carraway, his right hand and wrist swollen and sore from painting, surrenders to exhaustion. The starboard side of the *Troubador* is half white.

He goes to his cabin and writes:

Sweetheart, if you ever get to read this—and I wouldn't give a plugged nickel for your chances of ever seeing it— let me begin where I left off last Friday. It's not hard to tell that this is not going to be written well, as usual, for I'm tired. If there were a chance of sleeping I'd turn in and write this later, but I couldn't sleep on a bet tonight. Now, maybe after I write this and get my mind out of the whirl it's in. . . .

When Carraway awakens in early afternoon, his wrist and arm still aching from long hours with the paint brush, there is hardly a sound on the ship. He can hear the distant drumming of the pumps and generators down in the engine room, but there is no whirr from the engines. The ship has stopped and is lying to in the ice pack. Almost everyone on board is asleep.

He goes out and finds that one half of the ship, the starboard side, is now completely white, blending in with the surface of the sea around them, which is four fifths ice. No one is moving about on the other ships. They too are half white. Silence surrounds the small convoy.

At 5 P.M., Lieutenant Gradwell orders the *Troubador, Ironclad,* and *Silver Sword* to move out with him. They've rested in the ice long enough. Now they'll creep through it, exposing their white sides mostly to the east, the likely direction of Nazi air attacks.

Carraway makes another entry in his diary:

Instead of lying in the ice, we . . . work further east into it, and then south. Invaluable time might be saved. [We] have been steadily grinding into the ice. Sometimes north; sometimes east; then again south, when the going gets too heavy.

Frequently, the old hull rattles from stem to stern. Her beams creak. When we fail to dodge a really big floe we have to smack it head on. But the ice is getting thinner.

In spite of the grinding, bumping, and banging, it is far better to be safe aboard the *Troubador* than in some other merchantmen. A few minutes after six, a single German bomber swoops out of the clear sky toward the SS *Pan Atlantic* as she toils toward the entrance to the White Sea. A bomb hurtles down, and the ship rises out of the water from the force of a tremendous blast. Her bow drops off. High explosives were in the hold forward of the midship house. She sinks in less than five minutes, taking twenty-six men with her.

The next day, July 7, the SS *Alcoa Ranger* and the British merchantman *Hartlebury* are sunk too, with heavy loss of life.

CHAPTER 15

COMMANDO RAID

MIDNIGHT PASSES, AND THE LOGBOOK IN THE chartroom of the *Troubador* is changed to July 8. The radio has been silent for several hours, but then, at a few minutes past 1 A.M., it begins to crackle.

The Matson ship *Olopana*, steaming south along the coast of Novaya Zemlya, takes a single torpedo in her engine room, killing the watch below instantly. Her SOS is heard all across the Barents Sea. Earlier her captain attempted to rescue the crews of the SS *Washington*, SS *Bolton Castle*, and SS *Paulus Potter*. They refused help, believing that the *Olopana* would be sunk too. Their estimate was correct.

Hearing the *Olopana*'s distress signals, Captain Walter Lovgren of the SS *Winston-Salem* decides he's had enough. He aims his big freighter toward the coast of Novaya Zemlya, running into Obsiedya Bay below Matochkin Shar. He does not stop until the vessel crunches up on a sand bar.

Soon captain and crew are setting up camp in an abandoned lighthouse on the shore of the bay. Lovgren plans to "sit this war out," he says. He couldn't care less about getting his cargo through to Premier Stalin's armies.

At 3 P.M. on the same day, Ensign Carraway makes another entry in his diary:

> We have been running in a good fog for two days, headed for the western coast of a Russian island that sounds like a noise between a sneeze and a burp [Novaya Zemlya]. It runs in a northeast, southwest direction, and we are to follow the coast south to the Soviet mainland, then run due west to the mouth of the White Sea. The captain has had his first good sleep in bed since July 4th. . . . He has been admirable in the ice, standing in the bitter cold atop the flying bridge for a better view, giving commands by the hundreds to the men on the wheel. We were the only ship to go through the stuff without a bent bow or other damage.

At 1 A.M. the following day, they sight land, the northern tip of Novaya Zemlya. On the four ships every man awake studies the island. Although it looks as if no human being has ever walked on it, there is no better scenic view this early morning. Bleak and snow-patched, the island is completely barren.

Since midnight the *Ayrshire*'s radio operator has been trying unsuccessfully to contact Archangel, to inform the British naval liaison office there that "Gradwell's group" is intact and in need of information on Novaya Zemlya. Particularly, *are German forces on the islands?* Gradwell has reason to believe that the Germans occupied these outlying islands the previous year, establishing weather and communication outposts as they had done at Spitsbergen.

Carraway's diary notes:

Finding a small bay with deep water, we dropped anchor and planned a war conference for 9 A.M. For the first time since leaving Hvalfjördur, I slept without full gear on. Pajamas felt good.

In the morning, the captains and armed guard officers of the three merchant ships gather in the small officers' messroom of the *Ayrshire* to discuss their immediate future. Carraway takes a seat beside Captain Salvesen. Coffee is poured and the talk begins.

The captain of the *Silver Sword* is all for scuttling his ship now. He does not think it is possible to survive a crossing of the

White Sea in the face of German bomber attacks. The captain of the *Ironclad* does not disagree, though it seems his mind is not made up as to what they should do.

Carraway smiles inwardly and is pleased as Captain Salvesen speaks his mind. The pint-sized master is enraged at the idea of scuttling a ship—any ship. Heatedly he exclaims that he is going to Archangel or be sunk on the way. In broken English, he tells the other two masters that if they want to return to Iceland, to scuttle their ships—or do anything except sail to Archangel—they can do so without his company.

"Ay vill go alone," he says bluntly.

Lieutenant Gradwell is grinning broadly, for he has no intention of not delivering the ships to the safety of Matochkin Shar, if not to the Russian mainland. The lawyer's naval uniform is rumpled from days of wear, but he is properly dressed in coat and tie. In fact, no one has seen him without a coat and tie since leaving Iceland.

Carraway adds his opinion: "I'm a hundred percent with Captain Salvesen."

The weakening spirits of the other two captains are rallied, and they all reach a unanimous decision to sail at 6 P.M.

Carraway, much relieved, returns to the *Troubador* and sleeps until lunch. Then he takes a long bath, shaves luxuriously, and changes into clean clothes.

"Let's go get 'em," he writes.

By this time the *Ayrshire* is tied alongside the *Troubador* and taking on coal. She is down to a few tons, and Salvesen issues orders to give her every nugget she can hold. Many members of the trawler's crew have come aboard to eat. The little ship is low on food, and the British sailors are amazed at the quantity and quality of the merchantman's fare.

Lieutenant Gradwell calls over to Carraway, who is standing out on deck, to extend an invitation for a drink. He tells Carraway what they can expect at Matochkin Shar: "There is a radio station south of here, originally held by the Russians. But it might now be in German hands."

That is intriguing, Carraway thinks. No matter where they turn, there seems to be a problem.

Gradwell continues, "You know, we must get through to the Russian command for aid." Carraway agrees.

Then Gradwell comes straight to the point: "If Jerry has the station, would you be willing to try and assault it, and take it?"

Although it is a rather large request, Carraway replies that he would be willing to do it, and together they begin to work up a plan of attack. By four o'clock the plan is completed. Carraway, with young Dick Elsden, the executive officer of the *Ayrshire,* as second in command, will lead six or eight men on an assault of the radio station. They'll be armed with submachine guns removed from the Army tanks on the *Troubador*'s deck.

A few minutes later Carraway returns to the *Troubador,* and in his cabin he pauses to think: what is a South Carolina newspaperman doing on a Russian island near the North Pole? Why, that's easy to explain. He's going to lead a commando raid on a Nazi radio station!

At six o'clock, the anchors on all four ships are heaved up, on schedule, and Lieutenant Gradwell's private convoy gets under way again. While the ships creep out of the bay, Carraway, Wilds, and several other gunners open the last tank on deck and remove the submachine guns, the "Chicago pianos." For his group Carraway has selected three of his gunners plus several volunteers from the ship's crew, one of whom speaks both Russian and German.

They then remove one of the ship's .30-caliber Lewis machine guns and "field-strip" it, detaching the mountings so that it will be portable. The gun is heavy but it can be fired by supporting it on anything stationary.

The plan is for the man with the Lewis gun to fire from a center position to attract attention. Two parties of three men each, armed with the submachine guns, will then surprise the flanks and rush the objective—the radio station.

While it may not be an ideal commando plan, it appears to be workable. Carraway does not allow himself to think of its possible flaws. Instead, he busies himself collecting every single .45 bullet aboard the *Troubador* to provide ammunition for the Chicago pianos.

According to the plan, the raid will take place at about 4 P.M. the next day, July 10. Carraway goes to bed in the early morning hours, having put the final touches on preparations for the raiding party.

CHAPTER 16

DA! DA!

CARRAWAY AWAKENS ABOUT TEN O'CLOCK, GOES TO the bridge to take a quick look around, and finds the ships are still proceeding south at a good clip. Breakfast is next, but he barely finishes it before Gradwell signals to him to get the landing party ready and armed. They have reached Matochkin Shar almost five hours ahead of schedule.

As Carraway reads the message, he hears a long blast from the *Ironclad*'s whistle. The ship is steaming a few hundred yards ahead, on the starboard beam of the *Troubador*. As the ensign watches, the *Ironclad* seems to rise in the water and then stops dead. She has gone aground.

The *Ayrshire*, a half mile ahead, turns sharply to come to the aid of the *Ironclad,* while the *Troubador* and *Silver Sword* reduce speed and edge into a bay. Within a few minutes the

Ayrshire is aground too. What a great way to begin a secret commando raid, Carraway thinks.

Carraway's diary describes the next few hours:

The trawler [the Ayrshire] pulled off, went alongside the Ironclad and tried to jerk her loose. In the meantime, we pulled up close to shore, a few hundred yards from the rocky cliff on which the radio station perched, and dropped anchor. There was nothing to do but wait. An examination of the shore revealed heavy gun emplacements, a radio tower and various meteorological installations.

There is no way to determine if the radio station is in German or Russian hands, but the fact that no one has opened fire on them indicates to Carraway that they may be in friendly territory. Nonetheless Carraway has Wilds train the 4.50 on the station.

At 4 P.M., the *Ayrshire*, having freed herself, comes alongside the *Troubador* to discharge about half of the *Ironclad*'s crew. Among them is the grounded ship's gunnery officer, Ensign Carter, who immediately volunteers to join the commando party.

Carraway confers with Gradwell and Sublieutenant Dick Elsden for a moment, and then the raid party, numbering six from the *Troubador* and five from the trawler plus the three officers, enters a motor lifeboat for the short run to the beach.

In addition to the submachine guns, pistols, and hand grenades (from the tanks), the assault force carries an American-Russian dictionary and an American flag. Carraway has also thoughtfully added cartons of cigarettes and candy bars to the raiding equipment. If "Jerry" isn't at Matochkin Shar, whoever is may be more friendly puffing away on well-cured Virginia tobacco.

The boat pulls away in a heavy chop and stiff wind, making it difficult for Maurice Wilds to aim the Lewis machine gun toward the beach. In fact, the sea is so rough that Carraway almost misses the sight of a single man in a rowboat, bounding up and down in the waves, coming toward them.

In a moment the interpreter from the *Troubador* hails the man to ask him if he's Russian. Seeing a dozen guns aimed down his throat, he yells back frantically, *"Da! Da!"* It is the Russian word for "yes."

There is laughter as well as considerable relief in the commando boat as the Russian guides them to a safe landing on the beach. Once ashore they unload the guns and climb an almost vertical 50-foot cliff.

Inside the largest building of the remote Soviet installation, Carraway finds five Russian men, one woman, and three dogs. The interpreter speaks "low" dialect while the residents of

Matochkin Shar speak only a "high" dialect, so communication consists mostly of smiles and gestures. The Russian woman offers them coffee, sliced black bread, and fish egg pie. Carraway responds with the candy bars and cigarettes.

They return to the ships and hold another conference aboard the *Ayrshire*, deciding to stay at Matochkin Shar for a few days until they can get a message through to Archangel or Moscow requesting an escort for the last leg of the voyage across the White Sea.

Meanwhile Gradwell has another job to do. The Russians have reported seeing a lifeboat on the beach about 10 miles north of the station. Gradwell soon leaves to rescue any survivors.

"But I went to bed," Carraway writes. The "commando raid" is over.

CHAPTER 17

THE WHITE SEA, AT LAST

SNOW COVERS THE HILLS AROUND THE TINY
settlement of Lagerni on Novaya Zemlya. Though awesomely
bleak and cold, no port has ever looked more beautiful to the
crews of the surviving ships.

Carraway awakens at about 7 A.M. this July 11.

I went out on deck and we hadn't moved. But the Ironclad
*had managed to get herself free at high tide. A little later,
the* Ayrshire *came alongside towing a lifeboat, and signaled us to follow. So we upped anchor, heading up the
strait. As we rounded a bend, taking us behind a snow-
capped mountain, what should come into sight but a
United States Liberty ship, hiding too. I signaled the Liberty and asked her name, and nearly passed out. It was a*

135

ghost ship, by God. The Benjamin Harrison, *which I thought had gone down on the morning of July 3rd, first ship to be lost. Ensign Thompson, whom I'd given up for dead, was aboard. We exchanged greetings and I found that the ship that was lost that day was the* Christopher Newport, *not the* Benjamin Harrison. *It's breakfast time now.*

In the next hours Carraway and the others begin to learn more of what has happened in the past week. They are told that the incredible and determined Commodore Dowding had been plucked from the wet misery of a life raft by the HMS *Lotus,* along with other surviving crew members of the *River Afton.* Every inch crammed with survivors of several ships, the *Lotus* had scurried to Matochkin Shar, to discover five more PQ 17 vessels that had come through undamaged. Hiding in the strait had been the *El Capitan, Ocean Freedom, Samuel Chase, Hoosier,* and *Benjamin Harrison,* along with several naval escort ships. Dowding had quickly organized a small convoy to escort these vessels to Archangel. The *Ben Harrison* had gone along but had had to return to Matochkin Shar after being lost in the fog.

No one now at Matochkin Shar knows the fate of the rest of this group of ships, but all marvel at the sheer courage and durability of the elderly Commodore Dowding. (Only the

Samuel Chase and *Ocean Freedom* reached port. The *Hoosier* and *El Capitan* were sunk.)

As the seven-day running battle with the Luftwaffe and Ice Devil subs draws to an end, the full disaster begins to unfold in naval headquarters in Moscow, Washington, and London. Details are still few, and the general public does not know the story. Radio Berlin, monitored in London, is boasting endlessly of the staggering losses of PQ 17. The German war machine is jubilant.

The world doesn't know, either, of the lifeboats and rafts that are still drifting ashore on Novaya Zemlya, their occupants often more dead than alive. The crews of merchant ships that sank have somehow survived the intense cold and wet. Many men are frostbitten; others are suffering from burns or broken limbs. As they reach the safety of land, they start fires, build shelters, and forage for food, unaware that the *Troubador* group is anchored snugly close by at Matochkin Shar. The hungry men shoot gulls, or snare goslings by hand. None of them realize that help is less than a hundred miles away.

At Matochkin Shar the ships await Commodore Dowding's return from Archangel. Naval authorities in Moscow and Archangel now know that the *Troubador* and the other vessels are hiding in the strait. Dowding has one more job to do—bring them to safety!

With the morning of July 17 comes a surprise. Someone

shouts, "Look!" and the men on the deck of the *Troubador* scan west. The Russian tanker *Azerbaijan,* having survived the first mass attack on July 4, now steams slowly up the strait, escorted by a Soviet armed trawler and an icebreaker.

Carraway watches the *Azerbaijan* and wonders where she's been all this time. Her deck is buckled; the big hole in her hull is plainly evident. Somehow, though, she seems indestructible. She joins the other merchantmen of PQ 17 in Matochkin but stays her distance. The men shrug—typical Russians, they say. No one even seems to be very much interested in her female gunners now.

Finally, on the 19th, a warm, sunny day on Novaya Zemlya, Commodore Dowding arrives off the islands with three escort vessels. They sail north. Nothing of importance is spotted until they reach the vicinity of the intentionally grounded SS *Winston-Salem.* Then the British *Empire Tide,* having fled from a submarine into Moller Bay, is located. She has several hundred survivors aboard.

Soon Dowding's three naval ships are under way again, and cruise slowly into the entrance of Matochkin Shar on the morning of July 20. The commodore's final mission is to collect all the ships in the passage and herd them through the White Sea. His last conference concerning PQ 17 is held aboard the minesweeper *Poppy,* now his flagship. He briefs the masters on the conduct of the run to Archangel. Although it in no way resembles the easy, affable big conference held in the *River Afton* in Hvalfjördur in late June, Dowding is once more calm and confident.

About 2 P.M., the last ships—the *Troubador, Silver Sword, Ironclad, Benjamin Harrison,* and *Azerbaijan*—plus the escorts form up and depart for the Soviet mainland.

Lieutenant Gradwell's responsibility has passed to Commodore Dowding and the senior escort officer. So the mighty little *Ayrshire* takes up escort station not too far from the odd-looking half-white and half-gray trio of ships that are veterans of the ice fields off Spitsbergen. The lieutenant can look at the *Troubador, Silver Sword,* and *Ironclad* with great satisfaction. They are afloat, and not a man in any of them has been lost.

To the very end, the *Troubador* has problems. Engine trouble develops on the afternoon of the 21st, and the ship falls far behind, then slowly catches up as Captain Salvesen shouts insults down the brass speaking tube to Chief Engineer Ingebretsen.

The next day, six more British and Russian naval escort ships join the protective force for this final voyage of PQ 17. There is now tremendous firepower should the Luftwaffe or Ice Devil boats try again. They decline.

With a frustrated Captain Salvesen pacing the bridge, the *Troubador* falls behind again on the 23rd, and by late evening the convoy is 20 miles ahead of her. But this time three escorts sail comfortably nearby, idling along as Ingebretsen yells at his stokers to throw more coal into the fireboxes.

On Friday, July 24, Ensign Carraway begins the day's diary:

Well, we're here. Almost. There are still some few miles to go before we can tie up to a dock, but that's a minor matter now. The Russkis have the ship, and that's the important thing. The important part of this job is over. . . .

Of the thirty-five merchant ships that sailed in PQ 17, the *Troubador* reaches port last, docking at Molotovsk, near Archangel, in midafternoon on July 25. For this ship, and all the others involved, it has been quite a voyage. There are now nearly 1200 survivors of PQ 17 ashore in North Russia (including all those rescued on Novaya Zemlya), eating barley soup and black bread, sleeping in beds instead of on ice-coated boat thwarts. They are lucky to be alive.

Appropriately enough, Ensign Carraway and his armed guard crew spend all of July 26 cleaning the much-used .37-mm tank guns. Carraway wants them to be in first-class condition to hand over to the Russians. The delivery of the equipment was, after all, the purpose of the convoy.

The next day, a Soviet officer comes aboard to take possession of the *Troubador*'s cargo. Carraway is astonished when the officer becomes enraged on learning that the Army tanks have been entered, that the guns have been fired. His is clearly not a South Carolina brand of gratitude.

As usual, Captain Salvesen has a solution: "Vell, den, if dey don't like it, ve'll yoost drop de damn tings into de vadder." Furthermore, both Carraway and Salvesen inform the angry Russian officer of their solution. Of course, they have no intention of dropping the tanks into the water—but the Russian grasps the point.

A few hours later the tanks are lowered over the side, gassed up, driven around several times and then placed on a flatcar, soon to be on their way to the Russian front. Ensign Carraway and his gunners are on hand to watch the train pull out, thinking it might be rather nice to have those .37-mms on the return trip through the Barents Sea.

CHAPTER 18

THE CONTROVERSY

IN THE WAKE OF PQ 17, IT WAS INEVITABLE THAT there would be repercussions. Indeed, the charges and countercharges began even before Commodore Dowding sailed on his final mission to escort the remaining ships out of Matochkin Shar.

Premier Stalin's anger over the affair was quickly reflected by his admirals and by his ambassador in London, Ivan Maisky. Stalin brushed aside the fact that he had personally insisted on the Arctic route instead of the safer course through the Persian Gulf; that he had been the principal pressure point for the sailing of PQ 17; that the British Admiralty had advised against the Arctic route for convoys during the summer months.

Churchill, who, against Admiral Pound's warning, had

143

bowed to the joint pressure of both Stalin and Roosevelt to get "the ships moving," now found himself in the middle. It was not an unfamiliar position for the Prime Minister.

On July 15, he sent a memo to Pound:

I was not aware until this morning that it was the Admiral of the cruisers, Admiral Hamilton, who ordered the destroyers to quit the convoy. What did you think of the decision at the time? What do you think of it now?

At the time, of course, Pound was not aware of the decision, as he told Churchill in reply to the memo.

In his memoirs, the Prime Minister later was to say: "So strictly was the secret of these orders being sent on the First Sea Lord's authority guarded by the Admiralty that it was not until after the war that I learned the facts. . . ." However, it is believed that Churchill knew considerably more than he chose to admit.

On July 15 also, Churchill proposed to the Admiralty that PQ 18, due to sail soon, be canceled; that more fighting ships be brought to Scapa Flow to contain the remaining German surface units; that the enemy be engaged, not "run from." The Admiralty was very much in agreement on suspending the Arctic convoys during the summer, but smarted from the implication that the Royal Navy had "run" from the Germans.

Churchill then wrote Stalin on July 17, saying that the story of PQ 17 was incomplete, but that the British no longer wished to risk their Home Fleet east of Bear Island, where it could be brought under German attack from Norwegian airfields. He tactfully informed Stalin that PQ 18 had been canceled.

Stalin wrote back that Russian experts found it hard to understand and explain the order given by the British Admiralty that the escorting vessels of PQ 17 should return, whereas the cargo ships should disperse and try to reach the Soviet Union one by one without any protection at all. On the subject of halting the convoys, the angry Stalin replied:

I never expected the British government would stop dispatch of war materials to us just at the very moment when the Soviet Union, in view of the serious situation on the Soviet-German front, required these materials more than ever.

Crisis resulted from this one convoy and it was to hang over every other convoy to Russia until the end of the war. PQ 17 also entered into the future planning of almost every convoy to be sailed anywhere near enemy territory. Naval commanders gained a new respect for the order to scatter, and its possible penalties. PQ 17 was a bitter military lesson.

As Churchill prepared to go to Moscow and to visit Stalin

personally, to mollify him on this score and discuss other matters with him, a meeting was set between Russian representatives and Admiral Pound. The Russians had not been satisfied with the explanations they had been given.

On July 28, Pound met with Ambassador Maisky and Russian admirals in the office of Foreign Secretary Anthony Eden. The Soviet representatives were angry from the start. Nothing came of the meeting.

An investigation was already under way in the Admiralty, and not much came of that either. There was a larger war to be fought, and Churchill had already found his scapegoat in Admiral "Turtle" Hamilton. The mistakes were not laid at Admiral Pound's door.

Churchill would later write: "Admiral Pound probably would not have sent such vehement orders if only our British warships had been concerned." He then hinted that the two American cruisers in Hamilton's force might have "disturbed the poise with which he [Pound] was accustomed to dealing . . . in these heart-shaking decisions." In fact, the American cruisers apparently had little to do with the scatter decision.

Admiral Tovey's estimate of the affair, in his operations report on PQ 17, was that "the order to scatter the convoy had been premature; its results were disastrous." No one was inclined to argue either point.

Even on a higher level there was still confusion about the

events in the Arctic seas. When British Admiral A. B. Cunningham visited President Roosevelt in August, the first thing FDR asked about was PQ 17. The admiral was there to discuss the Allied invasion of Casablanca, in Africa. Sensibly he sidestepped the question of the convoy, pleading ignorance.

Although there was sailor talk on both sides of the Atlantic, and many rumors, the American and British publics did not learn of PQ 17 until September, when brief and inaccurate accounts appeared in newspapers. They could gather from the reports, however, that a disaster had occurred.

Official documents concerning PQ 17 were immediately classified "Top Secret," and personnel were warned not to discuss the events of the Barents Sea. To avoid embarrassment, the Admiralty managed to keep a blanket on the information until 1958. Obviously, it would have preferred to have the incident remain buried forever.

The American naval historian Samuel Eliot Morison wrote: "There has never been anything like it in our maritime history." The American Seamen's International Union called it "the most tragic episode of the war at sea." Never before had a convoy been completely abandoned at its moment of greatest peril, nor had any convoy in modern military history lost as many ships as PQ 17.

Yet military experts also point out that had the convoy not sailed and had no Allied supplies reached Russia through the icy ports of Murmansk and Archangel, the Soviet armies might well have fallen, altering the course of the war and perhaps the course of history. No political or military decision of any magnitude is simple or entirely safe.

Soviet troops finally drove the German Army out of Russia, and by 1943, the Allies had gained control of the sea lanes, including those off the coast of Norway. No further convoy disasters occurred. The supply chain of merchant ships to Russia and other parts of Europe grew stronger each year; the military equipment the ships carried eventually enabled the Allies to crush the enemy.

As for the mammoth battleship *Tirpitz,* the cause of all the trouble, she ventured out of the Norwegian fjords on only one other occasion, to take part in a futile and embarrassing raid against Allied transmitting stations on Spitsbergen. Meanwhile, she was attacked month in and month out by Allied aircraft, torpedo boats, midget submarines, and even a Norwegian fishing vessel. She remained a huge and painful steel thorn in the side of the Royal Navy. Finally, in September 1944, the famed "Dam Busters" of RAF Squadron 617 got her at Tromsö. Her magazine blew up, and the *Tirpitz* turned upside down.

The final accounting of PQ 17 was twenty-three ships lost, with a cargo capacity of 142,518 tons. Russia was deprived of more than 3,000 motor vehicles, 400 tanks, and 200 bombers. Only a quarter of the 188,000 tons of cargo in PQ 17 arrived in Archangel. Of the merchant crews, 153 seamen died. The German cost was a mere five aircraft.

There was another PQ 17 casualty—in London in 1943. The First Sea Lord, Sir Dudley Pound, died. The Admiralty listed the official cause of his death as "exhaustion." His widow told the *London Times:* "PQ 17 weighed heavily on the Admiral. It was very much a contributing cause toward his death."

The prominent *Manchester Guardian* put it another way: "PQ 17 killed the First Sea Lord."

ENSIGN CARRAWAY AND THE REST OF THE *TROUBADOR*'S
crew had little choice but to sail home from Russia in another
convoy, back over the same miserable seas. True to form and
personality, the *Troubador* fell behind the convoy in the White
Sea. For ten days she sailed alone, and as she neared Spitsbergen she was attacked by a German submarine. One torpedo
passed so close to the ship's stern that Carraway could see the
markings and copper bands on it. Shortly after the *Troubador*
transmitted a message that she was under attack, a plane from
a British carrier dropped a note saying that help was on the
way. When a British destroyer finally arrived, many of the
Troubador's crew broke down and wept openly. After staying
overnight in Low Sound on the main island of Spitsbergen and
undergoing an air attack, the *Troubador* sailed with a tanker,
this time accompanied by five British destroyers. The old

freighter arrived safely in Iceland and then continued on to America.

Carraway and his armed guard crew were detached from the ship on November 10, 1942, and began a well-deserved twenty-four days of leave. The crew members were then assigned to other merchant ships, and Carraway became an armed guard instructor at Little Creek, Virginia, a job for which he was now thoroughly qualified.

The SS *Troubador* continued to carry military cargoes throughout the war. After hostilities ended, she returned to her civilian capacity and regained her former name of *Confidenza*. The last shipping notation of her appeared in the mid-1950s; it is presumed that she then departed for the scrapyard after a long, useful, and very eventful life.

Bibliography

Blond, Georges. *Ordeal Below Zero*. London: Souvenir Press, 1956.

Campbell, Ian, and MacIntyre, Donald. *The Kola Run: A Record of Arctic Convoys, 1941–1945*. London: Frederick Muller, 1958.

Campbell, I. M. R. "Russian Convoys 1941–1945." *Royal United Service Institute Journal*, vol. 91 (May 1946).

"Convoys to North Russia." Supplement to *London Gazette*, October 13, 1950.

Irving, David. *The Destruction of Convoy PQ 17*. New York: Simon & Schuster, 1968.

Karig, Walter, et al. *Battle Report: The Atlantic War*. New York: Rinehart, 1946.

Karweina, Gunter. *Geleitzug PQ 17: Ein Tatsachenbereit*. Hamburg: Mosaik Verlag, 1964. (A firsthand account of PQ 17 from the German point of view.)

Lund, Paul, and Ludlam, Harry. *PQ 17—Convoy to Hell: The Survivor's Story*. London, New York: Foulsham, 1968.

Morison, Samuel E. *The Battle of the Atlantic 1939–1943*. Boston: Little, Brown, 1962.

Pope, Dudley. *73 North: The Defeat of Hitler's Navy*. New York: Lippincott, 1958.

Roskill, S. W. *The War at Sea, 1939–1945*. Vols. I through IV. London: H.M. Stationery Office, 1954.

Seafarers in World War II. New York: Seafarers International Union, 1947.

U.S. Navy Department. *Enemy Attack on Merchant Ships*. Washington, D.C.: 1942 (declassified 1958).

———. "Narrative by Howard E. Carraway." Washington, D.C. (declassified 1958).

Waters, John M. *Bloody Winter*. New York: Van Nostrand, 1967.

Winn, Godfrey. *PQ 17*. London: Hutchinson, 1947.

Woodward, David. *The Tirpitz and the Battle for the North Atlantic*. New York: Norton, 1954.

Index

ABOUT THE AUTHOR

"Lacking a good imagination, certainly unable to write science fiction, I must rely on personal experience, research and real characters to deliver my stories," noted award-winning author THEODORE TAYLOR.

Taylor's own life provided direct experience for a book about a dangerous convoy mission during wartime. He served in convoys during World War II as an able-bodied seaman aboard the merchant ships SS *Annibal,* SS *Exanthia,* and SS *Cape Avinof.* He also served aboard two United States Navy vessels: the USS *Draco* and the USS *Sumner.*

Taylor was born in rural North Carolina. His family was poor, and he spent much of his time outdoors, sometimes fishing with his father at the Hatteras Banks, a location that would become the backdrop to many of his stories.

Taylor did not begin writing books for young adults until 1968. His first novel for young readers, *The Cay,* is the story of a boy's life-threatening adventure at sea. *The Cay* won eleven literary awards and became a motion picture starring James Earl Jones. This immensely popular book has now sold over 4,000,000 copies worldwide.

BOOKS IN THIS SERIES

✹STERLING POINT BOOKS